ISBN 978-1-330-67731-5
PIBN 10091042

This book is a reproduction of an important historical work. Forgotten Books uses
state-of-the-art technology to digitally reconstruct the work, preserving the original format
whilst repairing imperfections present in the aged copy. In rare cases, an imperfection in
the original, such as a blemish or missing page, may be replicated in our edition. We do,
however, repair the vast majority of imperfections successfully; any imperfections that
remain are intentionally left to preserve the state of such historical works.

THE GERMAN AND SWISS SETTLEMENTS OF COLONIAL PENNSYLVANIA: A STUDY OF THE SO-CALLED PENN-SYLVANIA DUTCH

BY

OSCAR KUHNS

*Member of the Pennsylvania Society of the Sons of the
Revolution, of the Pennsylvania-German Society, and of
the Lancaster County Historical Society*

NEW YORK

HENRY HOLT AND COMPANY

1901

THIS BOOK IS DEDICATED BY THE AUTHOR
TO THE MEMORY OF HIS ANCESTORS

GEORGE KUNTZ

AND

HANS HERR

PIONEER SETTLERS OF
LANCASTER COUNTY, PENNSYLVANIA

" *Die Enkel gut thun an die Mühen
ihrer Vorfahren zu denken.*"
—FREYTAG.

PREFACE.

THE object of this book is to give a complete yet concise view of a too-much-neglected phase of American origins. The author has especially tried to be impartial, avoiding as far as possible mere rhetoric, and allowing the facts to speak for themselves. As a book of this kind can have no real value unless it is reliable, authorities have been freely quoted, even at the risk of making the number of foot-notes larger than is perhaps suited to the taste of the general public.

BERN, SWITZERLAND,
  October 1, 1900.

CONTENTS.

THE GERMAN AND SWISS SET-TLEMENTS OF COLONIAL PENNSYLVANIA.

CHAPTER I.

THE HISTORIC BACKGROUND.

OF all the great nations of Western Europe during the centuries immediately following the discovery of America, Germany alone took no official part in the colonization of the New World. Spain in Florida and South America, France in Canada and Louisiana, Holland in New York, England in Massachusetts and Rhode Island, and even Sweden in New Jersey, took formal possession of the territory settled by their subjects. Previous to the American Revolution it is estimated that over 100,000 Germans and Swiss settled in Pennsylvania alone, to say nothing of New York, Maryland, Virginia, Georgia, and the Carolinas. And yet this, for the times, extremely large immigration was not officially recognized by the home country, and the settlers themselves, instead of founding a German empire in the West, became at once the subjects of a foreign power.

Nor does it follow necessarily that the German character is not adapted to the work of colonization; at the present time Germany is at least trying to take her place in this kind of expansion, and the not-distant future may show her to be, in this as in other respects, no inconsiderable rival of England.[1]

One highly important cause of this emigration "without a head," as it has been called, was undoubtedly the demoralized condition of Germany in consequence of the terrible civil and religious wars that again and again swept over that country. As a final result of these wars the Holy Roman Empire was broken into fragments; one half of the German-speaking people were separated from their fellows and merged with Hungary and Bohemia to form Austria; while the

[1] Riehl, the great German ethnologist, is convinced of the colonizing power of his fellow countrymen,—the peasant classes at least: "Seine Ausdauer und Zähigkeit macht den deutschen Bauer zum geborenen Kolonisten, sie hat ihn zu dem grossartigen weltgeschichtlichen Beruf geweiht, der Bannerträger deutschen Geistes, deutscher Gesittung an allen Weltenden zu werden." (Die Bürgerliche Gesellschaft, p. 63.) John Fiske, however, gives as the only cause of England's supremacy in colonization the principle of self-government. (Dutch and Quaker Colonies, vol. i. p. 131.)

other half was split up into little kingdoms and principalities, whose chief efforts for nearly two hundred years were directed to recovering from the blighting effects of the Thirty Years' War.

But while the above-mentioned facts explain the lack of official German colonization, they also account for the enormous and almost spontaneous movement of emigration to America, and especially to Pennsylvania, at the beginning of the last century. The Pennsylvania German of to-day, who seeks to know why his ancestors came to this country some two centuries ago, must cast his eyes backward to the Reformation and the century and a half following thereupon.

The Thirty Years' War was one of the most destructive wars in history.[2] Not only were city, town, and village devastated in turn by the armies of friends as well as of foes; not only did poverty, hardship, murder, and rapine follow in the wake of these strange armies, with their multitudes of camp-followers; but the whole intellectual, moral, and religious character of the German people received a shock that almost threatened it with annihilation.[3]

[2] Cf. Freytag : " Dieser dreissigjährige Krieg, seit der Völkerwanderung die ärgste Verwüstung eines menschenreichen Volkes." (Bilder aus der deutschen Vergangenheit, vol. IV. p. 5.)

[3] " Man mag fragen, wie bei solchen Verlusten und so gründ-

Of all the classes which suffered the dire consequences of the Thirty Years' War, none suffered more completely than the peasants, or farmers. Before that event the yeomanry of Germany were in a state of great prosperity. Their houses were comfortable, their barns capacious, their stables well stocked with horses and cattle, their crops were plenteous, and many had considerable sums of money safely stored away against a rainy day;[4] some even boasted of silver plate.[5]

The outbreak of the religious wars in Bohemia was like the first faint rumble of the coming tempest, and before long the full fury of the storm of war broke over Germany itself. The sufferings of the country folk during the thirty years that followed are almost incredible. Freytag has furnished many details which are drawn from documentary sources, and yet which seem too heart-rending to be true. Not only were horses and cattle carried away by the various armies which shifted back and forth over the length and

lichem Verderb der Uberlebenden überhaupt noch ein deutsches Volk geblieben ist." (Freytag, vol. III. p. 115.) Freytag says that three things, only, kept alive the German nationality: the love of the people for their own homes, the efforts of the magistrates, and especially the zeal of the clergy. (p. 116.)

[4] See Freytag, III. pp. 103 ff.
[5] Illustrirte Geschichte von Würtemberg, p. 473.

breadth of the land; not only were houses, barns, and even crops burned; but the master of the house was frequently subjected to fiendish tortures in order that he might thus be forced to discover the hiding-place of his gold; or, as often happened, as a punishment for having nothing to give. At the approach of a hostile army the whole village would take to flight, and would live for weeks in the midst of forests and marshes, or in caves.[6] The enemy having departed, the wretched survivors would return to their ruined homes, and carry on a painful existence with the few remains of their former property, until they were forced to fly again by new invasions.[7] Many were slain, many of the young were lured away to swell the ranks of the armies, many fled to the cities for safety and never returned to their native villages. The country which had shortly before been so prosperous was now a wilderness

[6] For a vivid account of this life see W. O. von Horn, "Johannes Scherer, der Wanderpfarrer in der Unterpfalz." Of especial interest are the references to the sufferings of the times made by Yillis Cassel, who was the ancestor of the well-known Pennsylvania family of that name. Extracts are given in Cassel's Geschichte der Mennoniten, p. 431 ff.

[7] Johannes Heberle, a Swabian peasant, tells us in his diary that he was forced to fly thirty times: "Gott Lob und Dank wir sind diesmal noch gern geflohen, weil es die letzte Flucht war, die 29. oder ungefähr 30." (Würtembergische Neujahrsblätter, sechstes Blatt, 1889.)

of uncultivated land, marked here and there **by** the blackened ruins which designated the site of former farms and villages.

Freytag gives some most astonishing figures of the losses incurred. Taking as a sample the county of Henneberg (which he says was more fortunate than the other parts of Germany), he states that in the course of the war over 75 per cent. of the inhabitants were destroyed; 66 per cent. of the houses, 85 per cent. of the horses, over 83 per cent. of the goats, and over 82 per cent. of the cattle. It is a bloody story, says Freytag, which these figures tell. More than three-quarters of the inhabitants, more than four-fifths of their worldly goods destroyed. So complete was the desolation that it took two hundred years to restore the same state of agricultural prosperity.[8]

These facts are true to a still greater extent of other parts of Germany, and more especially of the Palatinate, which from its position was most exposed to the ravages of the contending armies.

[8] Following are some official statistics given by Freytag: In nineteen villages of Henneberg there were in the years

	1634	1649	1849
Families........	1773	316	1916
Houses.........	1717	627	1558

Similar statistics are given in regard to horses, cattle, etc. (Vol. III. p. 234.)

The Palatinate has a history at once interesting and important. Its inhabitants are the descendants of the group of German tribes called
the Rheinfranken, with an admixture of the Alemanni, the latter of whom had occupied the land
until 496 A.D., when Chlodwig, king of the
Franks, defeated them in a battle fought some-
where on the Upper Rhine.[9] They were and are
still among the best farmers in the world, in
many districts having cultivated the soil for thirty
generations.[10] Situated as they are along the
great water highway of Europe, they are said,
by those who know, to combine the best qualities
of North and South, being distinguished for indomitable industry, keen wit, independence, and
a high degree of intelligence.[11] During the Mid-

[9] The Alemanni afterwards settled in Swabia (Würtemberg)
and Switzerland.

[10] "Kraft dieser angestammten Lebensklugheit hat sich der
Franke in der Pfalz, am Mittelrhein und Untermain den Boden
dienstbar gemacht wie kein anderer deutscher Stamm." (Riehl,
Die Pfälzer, p. III.)

[11] Cf. Riehl, Die Pfälzer, and Häusser, Geschichte der Rheinischen Pfalz. Fiske says: "In journeying through it [what
he calls the Middle Kingdom] all the way from Strasburg to
Rotterdam, one is perpetually struck with the general diffusion
of intelligence and refinement, strength of character and personal dignity ; and there is reason for believing that at any
time within the past four or five centuries our impression would
have been relatively very much the same." (Dutch and
Quaker Colonies, I. p. 10.)

dle Ages the Palatinate had been among the
most powerful and influential of the German
states; it had rejoiced in great and enlightened
rulers like Conrad von Hohenstauffen, Frederick
the Wise (who recognized the Reformation), and
the tolerant and broad-minded Karl Ludwig, the
protector of the Swiss Mennonites. The country
along the Rhine and the Neckar was known as
the garden of Germany; the University of Heidelberg was one of the oldest and most influential seats of learning in Europe.

The terrible disorders of the religious wars dealt
a deadly blow at this prosperity and glory. It
was the Elector Palatine Frederick V. himself
who, by accepting the crown of Bohemia, pre-
cipitated the Thirty Years' War, and thus attracted to his own country the full fury of that
war. The horrors related above were repeated
here on a still larger scale. Häusser tells how, at
the capture of Heidelberg by Tilly in 1622, the
soldiers, not content with fire, plunder, and
rapine, pierced the feet of the wretched citizens
with nails, burned them with hot irons, and committed other similar barbarities.[12]

[12] At this time occurred the plunder of the celebrated library
of Heidelberg when the priceless manuscripts and books were
carried off to enrich the treasures of the Vatican. Napoleon
in his turn robbed the Vatican library, and in 1815 part of the
books and manuscripts stolen were returned to Heidelberg.

So again in 1634, after the defeat of the Swedes at Nördlingen, different bands of soldiers swept in their retreat over the Palatinate, utterly disregarding all law, mishandling persons and destroying property. Häusser says that the devastation of the land, just recovering from its former destruction, was beyond imagination. The cavalry of Horn and Bernard of Weimar left behind them terrible traces of plunder, destruction, and death; hunger, violence, and suffering were on all sides. The years 1635 and 1636 mark the period of the most terrible misery. In the years 1636-38 famine and pestilence came to add to the suffering. The people tried to satisfy hunger with roots, grass, and leaves; even cannibalism became more or less frequent. The gallows and the graveyards had to be guarded; the bodies of children were not safe from their mothers. So great was the desolation that where once were flourishing farms and vineyards, now whole bands of wolves roamed unmolested.

It might seem as if the above statements were extravagant or were mere rhetorical exaggerations. Yet these facts are given almost in the very words of a staid and judicious German historian.[13] For the North of Germany this state of affairs came practically to an end with the Peace of West-

[13] Ludwig Häusser, Geschichte der rheinischen Pfalz.

phalia in 1649, by which the political map of
Europe was finally settled and a condition of
toleration, at least, was agreed upon between the
three confessions—Catholics, Lutherans, and Reformed. For the Palatinate, however, the respite
was of short duration. By the terms of the peace
the Upper Palatinate was taken away and given
to the Duke of Bavaria, who also received the
title of Elector, while a new electoral title was
created for Karl Ludwig.

Under the wise administration of the latter
prince the land began slowly to recover from its
desolated condition; the banks of the Neckar and
the Rhine had become a desert; the vineyards
were gone, the fields covered with thorns; instead of the former flourishing villages a few
wretched huts were found here and there. Yet
so favored by Heaven is this fertile land that
the improvement was rapid. Many who had fled
returned; lands were plenty, taxes were light.
Other colonists came from Switzerland, Holland,
France,[14] and even England. The town of

[14] Among the founders of Germantown were certain Dutch
families from Kriegsheim, near Worms. (See Pennypacker.)
So also a number of the Huguenot settlers of both Pennsylvania
and New York were from the Palatinate. The settlement of
New Paltz in the latter State was so called by the French in
memory of the land which had been their home for many
years. (See Baird, The Huguenot Emigration to America.)

Frankenthal was almost entirely inhabited by these foreigners. Religion was free; Karl Ludwig was much more liberal than his predecessors had been. He was one of the first of German princes to discard the idea that in order to govern his subjects well they must all be of the same confession as himself. The Anabaptists, or Mennonites, who had lived for a number of years in the Palatinate, and had often been oppressed, now received from Karl Ludwig freedom of worship. Thus the country in a short time began to prosper anew. So great was the change that the French Field-marshal de Grammont, who in 1646 had passed through the devastated land, twelve years later was filled with amazement at the change, " as if no war had ever been there."

In the years 1674-75 the war between France and Holland, into which the Elector of Brandenburg and the Emperor Leopold had been drawn, brought destruction once more to the Palatinate —lying as it did between the two contending countries—and the painful efforts of twenty years remained fruitless. It was the purpose of Louis XIV. to render the Palatinate useless to his enemies. Turenne, who had received definite orders from Versailles to devastate the Palatinate, did his work thoroughly. Once more the

monotonous tale of misery must be told: nobleman, citizen, peasant plundered; fields laid waste;
cattle carried off; even the clothing torn from
the backs of the wretched victims. What could
not be carried away was destroyed; even the bells
and organs were taken from the churches. At
one time seven cities and nineteen villages were
burning; starvation once more threatened the
homeless peasant. This, however, was only the
prelude to the famous, or rather infamous, destruction of 1689.

In 1685 the Simmern-Zweibrücken dynasty
died out, and the Neuburg line, represented by
Philip William, inherited the electoral title of the
Palatinate. It was at this juncture that Louis
XIV. made his utterly unjust and unrighteous
claim to a large portion of the Palatinate in the
name of the daughter of the late Elector, Elizabeth,
who had married the Duke of Orleans, the disso-
lute brother of the French king. All this in spite
of the fact that Elizabeth had no legal right to the
land, and did not herself claim it. At this ef-
frontery on the part of Louis, all the princes of
Northern Europe leagued themselves against
him; England, Holland, and Germany stood as a
solid mass against the intrigues of France.
Louis—feeling his inability to cope single-handed

with this mighty coalition, and determined that " if the soil of the Palatinate was not to furnish supplies to the French it should be so wasted that it would at least furnish no supplies to the Germans "—approved the famous order of his war-minister, Louvois, to " brûler le Palatinat." The scenes that followed surpassed even the horrors of the Thirty Years' War. The recapitulation of such scenes only becomes monotonous and finally loses its effect on the imagination. Macaulay's description, however, is so vivid that we give a few extracts from it in this place. "The commander announced to near half a million human beings that he granted them three days of grace, and that within that time they must shift for themselves. Soon the roads and fields, which then lay deep in snow, were blackened by innumerable multitudes of men, women, and children flying from their homes. . . . Meanwhile the work of destruction went on. The flames went up from every market-place, every parish· church, every country-seat, within the devoted province. The fields where the corn had been sowed were ploughed up. The orchards were hewn down. No promise of a harvest was left on the fertile plains near what had been Frankenthal. Not a vine, not an almond-tree was to be seen on the slopes of the sunny hills round what had once been Heidelberg." [15]

During this trying period, the Reformed especially suffered; their churches were burned, or turned over to the Catholics; on both sides of the Rhine Prötestantism received a deadly blow. It was the desire of Louis not only to seize the country, but to crush out heresy there. The Elector Philip William, Catholic though he was, promised to help his oppressed people, but died before he could accomplish anything. He was even forced by the poverty of the land to dismiss many Protestant pastors, teachers, and officials, and to combine or to dissolve a number of churches and schools.

And here for the first time the religious condition of the Palatinate enters as an important factor in preparing the way for the movement of German emigration to Pennsylvania. Hitherto the province had enjoyed religious freedom. After the Lutheran Elector Otto Heinrich the land had a succession of Calvinist rulers, until the accession of the Neuburg line in the person of Philip William in 1685. It is true that Lutherans and Reformed had had many a bitter discussion and the former had often suffered injustice at the hands of their by far more numerous rivals.

[15] History of England, vol. III. p. 112.

But all this was trifling compared with the systematic oppression begun by John William[16] and continued by his successors for nearly a century.

Philip William, the first of the Catholic rulers of the Palatinate, was a kind-hearted, well-meaning man, by no means intolerant in matters of religion. His son and successor, however, was weak in character, and easily led by others. He had been educated by the Jesuits, and after becoming the ruler of an almost completely Protestant land he still retained the Jesuits as his political counsellors.

At the conclusion of hostilities between France and Germany, the Protestant church in the Palatinate was practically crushed. The French had everywhere supported the Catholics in their usurpations; the Reformed church-council was reduced to two men, and the Jesuits held full sway. In one place the Protestant inhabitants were compelled to share their church property with the Catholics; in another they were deprived of everything; before the end of 1693 hundreds of Reformed and a number of Lutheran churches were in the hands of the Catholic orders, to say nothing of the parsonages and schoolhouses.[17]

[16] Son of Philip William, who died in 1690.

[17] To add to their trouble a contest broke out at this time between the Reformed and the Lutherans, much to the satisfaction of the Catholics. (See Häusser.)

The Treaty of Ryswick in 1697, by which was ended the war between France and Germany, was of little benefit to the Protestants of the Palatinate. They were compelled to accept the *status quo* of the Catholic usurpations. On the basis of the clause to this effect in the treaty, colossal claims were made by the Catholics. In 1699 the French diplomatist brought a list of 1922 places, mostly in the Palatinate, which he claimed for the Catholics; if he had succeeded in carrying through his demands, Protestantism in the Palatinate would have received its death-blow.

It is very probable that John William had conspired with France, Rome, and the Jesuits against his Protestant subjects, in introducing into the Treaty of Ryswick the clause concerning the condition of the Protestants in his dominions, and thus became, as Häusser puts it, " Landesverrather " instead of " Landesvater." Henceforth in all that pertained to the Reformed Church he followed the tactics of his Jesuit counsellors. He seemed to care more to restore Catholicism than to restore the prosperity of the land. In 1697 he declared it as " an inconceivable mark of divine favor, which they must ever keep sacred, that the electorates of the Palatinate and of Saxony had again fallen into Catholic hands."

When John William in 1698 came back to his

dominion, the first time since its destruction, it was not to heal wounds, but to add new ones to the Reformed Church. The large majority of the inhabitants of the land were Reformed or Lutherans;[18] there were but few Catholics. Yet the Elector, with a show of tolerance, issued a decree to the effect that all churches should be open to the three confessions. This tolerance, however, was only apparent, inasmuch as, while the Protestants were obliged to give up part of their churches, the Catholics remained in undisturbed possession of their own. In this way alone two hundred and forty churches were opened to the Catholics. Other oppressive measures were enforced. The Protestants were required to bend the knee at the passing of the Host, and to furnish flowers for the church festivals of their rivals; while the work of proselyting was carried on publicly by the Jesuits, who had been called in for that purpose. The Swiss Mennonites, the Walloons, and the Huguenots, who for many years had found a refuge in the Palatinate, were now driven from the land; many went to Prussia, Holland, and America.

While no great oppression was publicly made,

---

[18] The Lutherans were not nearly so numerous, however; hitherto they had about forty churches under the supervision of the Reformed Church.

yet there was a constant system of nagging,—
what would now be called a pin-pricking policy.
Often they would be beaten for refusing to bend
the knee in the presence of the Host, and for refusing to share in Catholic ceremonies. Their
pastors were driven away or thrown into prison.
By one single decree seventy-five schoolmasters
were rendered penniless. Hundreds of petty persecutions on person and property were made.

It is a subject of legitimate pride on the part
of the descendants of these people to know that
they could not be crushed. The Reformed
Church of the Palatinate showed itself to be bold
and self-sacrificing; the various congregations
held firm and would not change in spite of violence; the pastors were unyielding—there is not
an example of one who was a coward or proved
untrue to his office. Häusser pays the following
tribute to the steadfastness of the Church in
those days of trial: " Earnestness and modera-
tion prevailed among the persecuted congregations; the terrible sufferings of war, and the petty
persecutions that followed the peace, were excellent means for purifying the morals, and since
the days of Frederick IV., the Protestants of the
Palatinate had not maintained so good a moral
conduct as in the ' Leidenjahren ' of the Jesuit
reaction." One effect of all this, however, was

the spread of pietism and mysticism, which manifested themselves in religious emotion. A pastor of Heidelberg, Henry Horch, founded a sect which looked for the end of the world as a release out of all their sorrows.[19] The great body of the people, however, although undoubtedly deeply affected by pietism, remained true to sound religion. These conditions prevailed throughout the whole of the eighteenth century. From time to time the Protestant rulers of Europe interfered, and promises would be made, only to be broken. It would be a tedious repetition to give further instances of this persecution; what has already been given may stand for what went on for nearly one hundred years.

To the above historical and religious conditions which prepared the way for emigration to America we must add the corruption, the tyranny, the extravagance and heartlessness of the rulers of the Palatinate; all through the eighteenth century their chief efforts seemed to be directed to a base and slavish imitation of the life of the French court. While the country was

[19] It was about this time that Kelpius came to Pennsylvania, there to await the coming of Christ. It was also only a short time later that Alexander Mack founded the sect of the Dunkards. For other examples of the pietistic spirit see Chapter VI.

exhausted and on the verge of ruin, costly pal-
aces were built, rivalling and even surpassing
in luxury those of France; enormous retinues
were maintained; while pastors and teachers
were starving, hundreds of court officers lived
in luxury and 'idleness. The burden of feudalism
still lay heavy upon the peasants; the chasm between them and the upper classes became more
and more widened. Down to the French Revolution the peasant and his children were forced
to render body-service, to pay taxes in case of
sale or heritage, to suffer the inconveniences of
hunting, and, above all, to see themselves deprived of all justice.[20]

Such a state of things became intolerable. As
Häusser says, " In this way a part of the riddle
is explained which seemed so mysterious to the
statisticians of that time, i.e., why precisely in
these years of peace the population of the Palatinate diminished so surprisingly. Schlözer was
astonished at the fact that from no land in the
world relatively so many people emigrated as
from this paradise of Germany, the Palatinate.
A glance at the fatherly government of this paradise will give us the key to the riddle. Many
hundreds allowed themselves to be lured to
Spain (in 1768), where they were promised tol-

[20] Cf. Freytag, vol. III. pp. 427 ff.

erance. By way of England so many were shipped to America that for a long time the name of Palatine was used as a general term for all German emigrants."

In the above pages we have gone somewhat into detail in regard to the condition of affairs in the Palatinate, inasmuch as that province furnished by far the largest contingent of the German emigration to Pennsylvania. Many of the statements made, however, apply equally to Würtemberg, Zweibrücken, and others of the petty principalities in the neighborhood of the Palatinate.[21] The whole of South Germany had suffered from the Thirty Years' War, hence the same conditions which led to emigration— poverty, tyranny, and religious intolerance—existed everywhere, each province having in addition its local causes.

There is one country, however, which furnished a very large contingent to the emigration to Pennsylvania, and which was free from the

[21] One or two facts will illustrate the condition of Würtemberg after the Thirty Years' War. Before that event Stuttgart had 8200 inhabitants ; in less than two years 5370 had died ; the total population of the land in 1634 was 414,536 ; in 1639 there were not 100,000. (Illust. Geschichte von Württemberg, p. 512.) For a graphic description of the destruction of Zweibrücken see Heintz, Pfalz-Zweibrücken während des dreissigjährigen Krieges.

horrors of the Thirty Years' War. That is
Switzerland. To a certain degree this war was
for that country a blessing. Untouched themselves, the Swiss received thousands of fugitives
from the neighboring lands. This influx of people
raised the price of land and brought about a veritable " boom." The contrast between unhappy
Germany and peaceful Switzerland is thus graphi-
cally portrayed by a German traveller: " I then
came to a land where there was no fear of enemies
or of being plundered, no thought of losing life
and property; where every one lived in peace
and joy under his own vine and fig-tree; so
that I looked upon this land, rough as it seemed,
as an earthly paradise."[22] The devastation of
war, then, did not prepare the way for later emigration in Switzerland as it had done in South
Germany; and yet real and sufficient causes for
this emigration existed. While Switzerland has
ever been regarded as the ideal land of freedom,
it was, after all, up to the present century, but
little more than an aristocracy. The emoluments
of office in such cities as Berne and Zürich
were in the hands of a few patrician families,
which, generation after generation, held all
offices.[23] The lower classes, those who tilled

[22] Dändliker, Geschichte der Schweiz, II. p. 694.
[23] This was especially true of the eighteenth century ; cf.

the soil and who labored with their hands, had no share in the government and but little real freedom. The feudal system, which had existed for a thousand years in Switzerland, was not abolished till the French Revolution swept it away with many other relics of the past. During the period which we are studying, tithes, land-tax, body-service, and all the other accompaniments of the feudal relations between peasant and lord flourished apparently as vigorously as ever.[24] Add to this the traffic in soldiers which forms so deep a blot on the fair name of Switzerland, and which was a constant source of discontent among the people,[25] and we may have some idea of the secular causes of Swiss emigration during the last century.

Dändliker, II. pp. 632 and 710; III. p. 30: "Von freiem Verfügungsrecht der Gemeinden, von freier Wahl der Gemeindebehörden war noch keine Rede"; and again: "Allgemein war ferner jener Zeit eigen: der Zug zur Aristokratie. Allerorten häufte sich die Gewalt, tatsächlich oder Verfassungsgemäss, in den Händen Weniger."

[24] Dändliker, III. p. 33: "Das Feudal- oder Lehenswesen, ... volle tausend Jahre lang hatte es sich als Grundlage der Staats- und Gesellschaftsordnung erhalten können. ... Es behauptete noch immer seine volle Herrschaft in wirthschaftlichen und socialen Verhältnissen, zum Teil auch in der Staatsorganisation."

[25] At the end of the War of the Austrian Succession (1740) no fewer than seventy to eighty thousand Swiss soldiers were in foreign service; and the same number took part in the Seven Years' War (1756–63). (Dändliker, III. p. 19.)

The chief cause, however, of the earliest Swiss emigration to Pennsylvania was of a religious nature. We shall have occasion later to speak of the origin of the Mennonites, who form so striking a feature of the religious life of the Pennsylvania of to-day. During the fifteenth and sixteenth centuries the annals of Berne and Zürich contain frequent references to the measures taken to root out this sect, many of whose doctrines were distasteful to the state churches founded by Zwingli, especially their refusal to bear arms.[26] From their first appearance in Switzerland in the early decades of the sixteenth century, the Mennonites were the victims of systematic persecution on the part of their Reformed brethren; even the death-penalty being inflicted on a number, while others were thrown into prison, exiled, or—in the case of a few—sold to the Turks as galley-slaves.

From time to time single families and individuals had fled across the frontiers and sought

[26] This is frequently given as the reason for Berne's severity against the Menonnites. Thus the Bernese ambassador or agent in Holland excused the persecution of the Mennonites on the ground that the only possibility of defending a state depended on the power of the sovereign to call the subjects to arms in case of need, etc. (Müller, Geschichte der Bernischen Täufer, p. 260.)

refuge in the Palatinate, where Mennonite communities had existed since 1527. In 1671 the first considerable emigration took place, when a party of seven hundred persons left their native land and settled on the banks of the Rhine. These were afterwards the supporters of their compatriots, who willingly or unwillingly left Switzerland in the following years. These Palatine Swiss had to suffer the same trials as their neighbors, but were treated with even more intolerance. Poverty, floods, failure of crops, the billeting of foreign soldiers, all contributed to make their lot intolerable, and finally induced large numbers of them to join their brethren in Switzerland in the movement which resulted in the settlement on the Pequea in Lancaster County.

The above-mentioned causes, both secular and religious, produced a widespread discontent and fostered the prevalent desire for emigration in Switzerland.[27] That it reached important dimensions may be inferred from the fact that Zürich passed decrees against it almost annually

[27] "Die Armut in manchen Gegenden und dazu die plötzlich eintretenden Notzeiten zwangen jetzt im achtzehnten Jahrhundert zuerst die Schweizer zur Auswanderung. Vereinzelt war diese zwar schon im siebzehnten Jahrhundert vorgekommen, wurde aber erst jetzt häufiger und allgemeiner." (Dändliker, vol. III. p. 186.)

from 1734 to 1744; even Berne, which had previously sent Michel and Graffenried to prepare
the way for a Swiss colony in Georgia, changed
its policy, and in 1736 and 1742 published decrees
forbidding emigration.[28]

In the preceding pages we have endeavored to
give the historical events and social conditions
which form the background to German emigration to Pennsylvania, and without which that
emigration would never have taken place. Of
course in addition to these there were many
other direct and indirect causes, such as Penn's
travels to Germany,[29] and the pamphlets descrip-
tive of his " Holy Experiment," which he afterwards caused to be published in English, Dutch,
and German, and which were scattered broadcast
over South Germany. So, too, the efforts of
Queen Anne and her Golden Book, which
brought that flood of Palatines to London, in
1709, out of which were to come the settlements
on the Schoharie and the Mohawk, and later
those on the Tulpehocken, in Berks County,

[28] See Good, The German Reformed Church in the United
States, p. 172. Speaking of the party which left Zürich in
1732, Salomon Hess, one of the pastors of that city says :
"There was no good reason at that time for them to leave
their fatherland, but they were seized by an insane desire to
go to America." (Dubbs, Ger. Ref. Ch. p. 253.)

[29] See Chapter II.

Pa. George II. also published proposals aimed directly at the Mennonites in the Palatinate.

As in all other affairs of life, so in this matter of emigration, personal work undoubtedly did much. We know that when the Mennonites settled in Lancaster County, their first care was to send one of their number back to the Old World, in order to bring over their friends and brethren. We read in Christopher Sauer's letter to Governor Denny in 1755: "And when I came to this province, and found everything to the contrary from where I came from, I wrote largely to all my friends and acquaintances of the civil and religious liberty, privileges, etc., and of the goodness I have heard and seen, and my letters were printed and reprinted, and provoked many thousand people to come to this province, and many thanked the Lord for it and desired their friends also to come here." [30]

Speculation, too, entered as a powerful stimulant to emigration. As soon as the ship-owners saw the large sources of profit in thus transporting emigrants, they employed every means of attracting them. Thence arose the vicious class of "Newlanders" described in Chapter III.

Such are some of the leading causes of pre-

[30] Brumbaugh, A History of the Brethren, p. 377.

Revolutionary German emigration to Pennsylvania, general and particular, direct and indirect. But even all these causes might not have been effective were it not for the innate propensity to emigration of the German character, that "Wanderlust" (so strangely combined with love for home and country) that has been the distinguishing trait of German character from the dawn of their history down to the present.[31] It was this trait which has ever led them to leave their native country when scarcity of land, social and religious conditions, famine and war have furnished the immediate occasion. It was this which led to the vast movement of the "Völkerwanderung" in the fourth and fifth centuries, and to the colonization of Prussia and Silesia in the thirteenth and fourteenth centuries;[32] it was this that in our own century has sent successive waves of German immigrants to populate the Western States; it was this that in the eighteenth century sent the Palatines and Swiss to Pennsylvania, there to take root, and to build new homes for themselves and their

[31] "Die Liebe zur Heimath und daneben der unerhörte Wandertrieb." (Freytag, vol. I. p. 60.)

[32] "Seit in den Kreuzzügen der alte Wandertrieb der Deutschen wieder erwacht war, und Hunderttausande von Landleuten mit Weib und Kind, mit Karren und Hunden nach dem goldenen Osten zogen." (*I*bid., vol. II. p. 157.)

eir children's children. How
ded in this we shall try to show
chapters.

CHAPTER II.

THE SETTLING OF THE GERMAN COUNTIES OF PENNSYLVANIA.

IT would be an interesting and certainly a valuable thing to study in detail all the facts concerning the whole subject of German immigration to America, or even such immigration in the eighteenth century. There were colonies in New York, New Jersey, Maryland, Virginia, Georgia, Louisiana, North and South Carolina, and even so far north as Maine and Nova Scotia.[1] The German settlements in Pennsylvania, however, were more numerous and more important than those of all the other States combined. In the other States the Germans formed but a small percentage of the population, and have influenced but little the character of the State development; while those in Pennsylvania have from the beginning down to the present day formed at least one-third of the population, and have undoubtedly exercised a profound in-

[1] For books on this subject see Bibliography.

fluence on the development of the Quaker Commonwealth and of the neighboring States, especially those to the south and west. Many of the facts cited in this book apply equally well, however, to the Germans of New York, Maryland, Virginia, etc.[2]

In the present chapter an effort is made to give a general view of the streams of immigration which flowed into Pennsylvania between the years 1683 and 1775. We may divide this period into three parts: first, from 1683 to 1710, or from the founding of Germantown to the coming of the Swiss Mennonites; second, from 1710 to 1727, the year when the immigration assumed large proportions and when official statistics began to be published; the third period extends to the outbreak of the Revolution, which put an end to all immigration for a number of years.[3] During the first of the above periods the numbers were very small; the second period marks a considerable increase in

[2] Indeed in common parlance the expression "Pennsylvania Dutch" includes the Germans of Maryland and Virginia. Those in New York are often confused with their Holland neighbors, both by themselves and others.

[3] This book does not contemplate the discussion of German immigration after the Revolution ; for this phase of the subject see Löher, Geschichte und Zustände der Deutschen in Amerika, and Eckhoff, In der neuen Heimath.

numbers, which during the third period swell to enormous size.

The Pennsylvania Germans may be said to have a Mayflower, as well as the Puritans. In the year 1683 the good ship Concord (surely an appropriate name when we consider the principles of peace and harmony which marked Penn's "Holy Experiment"!) landed at Philadelphia,—then a straggling village of some fourscore houses and cottages,[4]—having on board a small number of German and Dutch Mennonites from Crefeld and Kriegsheim. With this little group the story of the Pennsylvania Germans begins. In order to understand why they thus came to the New World, we shall have to note some important religious movements which characterized the seventeenth century.

The Reformation in England gave rise to as many sects and parties as it did on the Continent. We may find an analogy between the Lutheran Church and the Church of England; between the Reformed (or Calvinists) and the Puritans (or Presbyterians); and between the Anabaptists or Mennonites and the Quakers and Baptists. This analogy is no mere fancy; we

[4] Proud, I. 263. "Such as they are," adds Penn, who gives these figures in a letter to the Free Society of Traders in London.

know the influence of Calvin on Puritanism; the Hanoverian kings of England were both Lutherans and Churchmen (the former in their private, the latter in their official capäcity); and modern Church historians have declared that it was from the Mennonites that the General Baptist Church in England sprang; while Barclay says of George Fox, the founder of the Quakers, "We are compelled to view him as the unconscious exponent of the doctrines, practice, and discipline of the ancient and stricter party of the Dutch Mennonites." [5] Thus, in the words of Judge Pennypacker, "to the spread of Mennonite teachings in England we therefore owe the origin of the Quakers and the settlement of Pennsylvania." [6]

When William Penn became a Quaker he was filled with missionary fervor; among his other labors in the field of missions he made two journeys to Holland and Germany. The second journey was made in 1677 and was fraught with momentous consequences for the subject which we are discussing. On July 26th of the above year, Penn with several friends—among whom were the well-known George Fox, Robert Barclay, and George Keith—landed at Briel in Holland, hav-

[5] Religious Societies of the Commonwealth, p. 77.
[6] The Settlement of Germantown, p. 66.

ing as their object " to extend the principles and
organization of the Quakers in Holland and Germany." It was not the first time that such efforts
had been made; as far back as 1655 William
Ames had established a small Quaker community at Kriegsheim, near Worms, in the Palatinate; and later William Caton, George Rolf,
Benjamin Furley,[7] and others had visited the
Palatinate.

Penn's visit to Germany coincided with the
great pietistic movement in that country.[8] The
causes of this movement are partly to be sought
in the wretchedness and sufferings of the times,
and partly in the stiff formalism into which the
Church had fallen. The comfort and satisfaction that could not be found in Church and
State were sought for in personal communion
with the Holy Spirit. Men turned from the cold-
ness of dogmatic theology to the ecstasies of religious emotion. In the words of Spener, the
great apostle of pietism, religion was brought
" from the head to the heart." This movement
spread in a great tidal wave of excitement over

[7] Furley afterwards became Penn's agent and played an important part in inducing German emigration to Pennsylvania.

[8] Penn himself says: "And I must tell you that there is a
breathing, hungering, seeking people, solitarily scattered up
and down the great land of Germany, where the Lord hath
sent me." (Works, London, 1726, vol. I. p. 69.)

Germany, Switzerland, Denmark, Sweden, and even England. The " collegia pietatis," or the meetings for the study of the Bible,—one might call them adult Bible-classes,—were held everywhere.[9] It was to friends in the spirit, then, that Penn came. He was everywhere welcomed by kindred souls, and their meetings were deeply marked by the outpouring of the Holy Spirit.[10]

The places visited by Penn which are of interest to us in our present discussion are Frankfort-on-the-Main, Kriegsheim, near Worms, on the Upper Rhine, and Mülheim-on-the-Ruhr; I have not been able to find any evidence that he visited Crefeld,—a city not far from the frontiers of Holland,—from which, as well as from Mülheim, the earliest settlers of Germantown came.

Penn reached Frankfort on August 20th, and there met a number of pietists, among whom were Dr. Wilhelm Petersen, his wife Johanna

[9] This was not a movement of secession from the established churches ; among the pietists were Lutherans, Reformed, and even Catholics. Spener was a Lutheran and opposed to sectarianism. For an interesting summary of pietism see Freytag. One of the well-known literary results of it is Jung-Stilling's Lebensgeschichte.

[10] He tells how at Frankfort " people of considerable note, both of Calvinists and Lutherans," received them " with gladness of heart and embraced our testimony with a broken and reverent spirit." (Works, vol. I. p. 64.)

Eleonora von Merlau,[11] Daniel Behagel, Caspar Merian, Johann Lorentz, Jacob van de Wall, and others, who afterwards became the founders of the Frankfort Company, and thus the fautors of German emigration to Pennsylvania. Their names certainly deserve to be remembered.

After leaving Frankfort, Penn went to Kriegsheim, where, as before stated, a little company of German Quakers had held together since the visit of Ames and Rolf, some twenty years before. Here, as he tells us in his Journal,[12] he found, to his great joy, a " meeting of tender and faithful people," and, after writing a letter to Karl Ludwig on the danger of religious intolerance, he returned to Holland and England.

In 1681 Penn received from Charles II., in payment of a debt of £16,000 sterling which the government owed his father, Admiral Penn, the grant of an immense tract of territory, situated between New Jersey and Maryland,[13] to which the king—against Penn's own wishes, however

[11] For interesting autobiographical extracts from the Lives of both Petersen and his wife see Freytag, Bilder aus der deutschen Vergangenheit, vol. IV. pp. 29 ff.

[12] Works, vol. I. p. 72.

[13] The indefinite language in which this grant was couched led afterwards to long disputes between Pennsylvania and Maryland, and was the occasion of the contest known as Cresap's War, in which the Germans of the present county of York took a prominent part.

—gave the name of Pennsylvania. Penn immediately planned what he called a " Holy Experiment " in government, a State in which religious as well as political freedom should be granted to all. He went about at once to attract colonists to his new colony, and soon after the formal confirmation of the king's grant there appeared in London a slender pamphlet entitled " Some Account of the Province of Pennsylvania in America," in which the advantages of the new State were set forth in a favorable light. Almost at the same time a German translation was published in Amsterdam, entitled " Eine Nachricht wegen der Landschaft Pennsylvania in America." [14]

Francis Daniel Pastorius, who may be called the Bradford of the Germantown settlement, writes in an autobiographical memoir as follows: " Upon my return to Frankfort in 1682 " (he had been travelling extensively through Europe, chiefly for pleasure), " I was glad to enjoy the company of my former acquaintances and Christian friends, Dr. Schütz, Eleonora von Merlau, and others, who sometimes made mention of William Penn of Pennsylvania, and showed me letters from Benjamin Furley, also a printed re-

[14] The same translation was published in Frankfort in 1683, as part of a larger work, " Diarium *Europæum*."

lation concerning said province; finally the whole secret could not be withholden from me that they had purchased twenty-five thousand acres of land in this remote part of the world. Some of them entirely resolved to transport themselves, families and all.[15] This begat such a desire in my soul to continue in the society, and with them to lead a quiet, godly, and honest life in a howling wilderness, that by several letters I requested of my father his consent."

In the mean time the Quakers and Mennonites of Kriegsheim had heard of the wonderful possessions of the quiet and gentle Englishman who had visited them a few years before, and had read how under his laws liberty of conscience was promised to all who should settle in the new colony. Comparing this prospect with their own unhappy condition, they immediately resolved to seek relief in Penn's land.[16]   By this time Pastorius had received the consent of his father (together with a sum of money), and thereupon went to

[15] None of them, however, did this.

[16] Their motives were undoubtedly identical with those thus expressed by Pastorius : "After I had sufficiently seen the European provinces and countries and the threatening movements of war, and had taken to heart the dire changes and disturbances of the Fatherland, I was impelled, through a special guidance from the Almighty, to go to Pennsylvania," etc. (Pennypacker, Settlement of Germantown, p. 75.)

Kriegsheim, where he saw the leaders of the intending settlers, Peter Schumacher, Gerhard Hendricks, and others, and with them discussed the preparations necessary for the long journey. He then descended the Rhine to Crefeld, where he conferred with Thones Kunders, Dirck Herman, the Op den Graeff brothers, and others, who followed him across the ocean six weeks later.

Pastorius thus became the agent of the Frankfort Company, of the Kriegsheimers and of the Crefelders. He sailed ahead of the others, June 6, 1683, and arrived in Philadelphia August 16, where he was heartily welcomed by Penn.[17]

[17] Francis Daniel Pastorius was no ordinary man ; indeed it is probable that there were few men in America at that time equal to him in learning. He was born in Sommerhausen, Germany, Sept. 26, 1651, studied at the Universities of Strasburg, Basel, Erfurt, Jena, and Altdorf, taking a degree in law at the latter place in 1675. Soon after he travelled in Holland, England, France, and Switzerland, bringing up at Frankfort in 1682, as noted above. He was well acquainted with Greek, Latin, French, Dutch, English, Italian, and Spanish, as may be seen from his commonplace-book written macaronically in these various languages and entitled the "Beehive." Extracts from this book have been published in the Americana Germanica. See also Pennypacker, pp. 109–114. Pastorius built for himself a small house, over the door of which he wrote : "Parva domus sed amica bonis: procul este profani." Whereat, he says, "Unser Gouverneur, als er mich besuchte, einen Lachen aufschluge und mich ferner fortzubauen anfrischete." (Beschreibung von Pennsylvanien, ed. by Kapp, p.

Pastorius was the advance courier of the prospective settlers of Germantown. July 24th thirteen men together with their families sailed for the New World on board the Concord, reaching Philadelphia October 6, 1683, some two months after Pastorius himself.[18] A short time thereafter all hands were busy getting settled for the winter in the new colony, then separated from Philadelphia by a stretch of primeval forest broken only by a narrow bridle-path.

23.) Whittier wrote what he considered his best poem, "The Pennsylvania Pilgrim," on Pastorius:

"Simply, as fits my theme, in homely rhyme
I sing the blue-eyed German Spener taught," etc.

(Works, vol. I. pp. 322 ff.)

[18] One single American poet has devoted a few lines to the arrival of this band of German pilgrims. In Whittier's "Pennsylvania Hall" the following lines are found.

"Meek-hearted Woolman and that brother-band,
The sorrowing exiles from their " Fatherland."
Leaving their home in Kriesheim's bowers of vine,
And the blue beauty of their glorious Rhine,
To seek amidst our solemn depths of wood
Freedom from man and holy peace with God;
Who first of all their testimonial gave
Against the oppressor, for the outcast slave.
Is it a dream that such as these look down
And with their blessings our rejoicings crown?"

(Works, vol. III. p. 58.)

The reference in the eighth and ninth lines is to the protest against slavery made to the monthly meeting of the Quakers, April 18, 1688, by Pastorius, Gerhard Hendricks, and the two Op den Graeff brothers. Pennypacker (p. 197) has reprinted this most interesting document.

Pastorius was no mere dreamer, but an active and able man. Under his supervision the land was soon cleared, houses built, and a prosperous community founded. That they had many hardships to suffer at first goes without saying. Arriving so late in the year, they had only time to build cellars and huts in which " they passed the year with much hardship." Pastorius says people made a pun on the name of the settlement, calling it " Armentown," because of lack of supplies. " It could not be described," he continues, " nor will it be believed by coming generations, in what want and need and with what Christian contentment and persistent industry the German township started."

Yet this state of want soon gave way to one of comparative comfort. On October 22, 1684, William Streypers (who had written to his brother the year before for provisions), writes: " I have been busy and made a brave dwelling-house, and under it a cellar fit to live in; and I have so much grain, such as Indian corn and buckwheat, that this winter I shall be better off than I was last year." October 12th of the same year Cornelius Bom wrote to Rotterdam: " I have here a shop of many kinds of goods and edibles. Sometimes I ride out with merchandise, and sometimes bring something back, mostly from the Indians, and deal with them in many ways. . . . I have no rent or tax or excise to pay. I have a cow which gives plenty of milk, a horse to ride around; my pigs increase rapidly, so that in the summer I had seventeen, where at first I had only two. I have many chickens and geese, and a garden, and shall next year have an orchard, if I remain well, so that my wife and I are in good spirits."

We have dwelt thus in detail on the settlement of Germantown, on account of its importance as the pioneer of all German settlements in America. Moreover, we are fortunately in condition, owing to the labors of Seidensticker and Pennypacker, to follow the movement, step by step, from its first inception in the old Kaiserstadt on the banks of the Main to the infant city of Brotherly Love in the New World. The rest of this chapter must be given more briefly.

Letters like the above undoubtedly influenced others to emigrate, for we read in the annals of the settlement of new arrivals every year. The only considerable addition, however, which we find in the last years of the century was in 1694, when an interesting band of mystics, forty in number, settled on the banks of the Wissahickon, under the superintendence of Johann Kelpius, a

man of great learning, though full of vagaries.[19]
Their object in coming to the New World was to
await the coming of the Lord, which they firmly
believed would occur at the turn of the century.
In their hermitage on the banks of the Wissahickon they cultivated physical and spiritual per-
fection, studied and taught;[20] among other

[19] Arnold (Kirchen- und Ketzer-Historie, vol. II. p. 1104),
under the heading "Mehrere Zeugen der Wahrheit," speaks
as follows : "Heinrich Bernard Cöster, Daniel Falckner, Joh.
Kelpius und M. Peter Schäffer samt andern die nach Pensyl-
vanien gezogen, Briefe und Schrifften aus America zu uns
übergesandt samt ihrem tapffern Gläubens-Kampff, und wie
sie sich durch alle Secten herdurch geschlagen um die Frey-
heit in Christo zu erhalten."

The real leader of this colony, however, was Joh. Jacob
Zimmermann,—"ein grundgelehrter Astrologus, Magus, Ca-
balista und Prediger aus dem Würtembergerlande," who had
resolved to forsake "das undankbare Europam" and with wife
and family and forty companions to go to America, but who
died at Rotterdam on the eve of his departure. (Arnold,
vol. II. p. 1105.)

Whittier (in his "Pennsylvania Pilgrim") speaks of

"Painful Kelpius from his hermit den
By Wissahickon, maddest of good men,
Dreamed o'er the chiliast dreams of Petersen."

[20] We get a glimpse of the character and the ideals of these
men in the following words written by one of them : "What
pleases me here [Pennsylvania] is that one can be peasant,
scholar, priest, and nobleman at the same time." "To be a
peasant and nothing else is a sort of cattle-life; to be a scholar
and nothing else, such as in Europe, is a morbid and self-
indulgent existence." (Penn. Mag., vol. XI.) There is a singular

things they built an astronomical tower, from which they kept constant watch for the signs of the coming of Christ.[21] This community lasted only a few years, its logical successor being the Ephrata community.[22]

The second period begins with the advent of the Swiss Mennonites in 1710. This movement without doubt is closely connected with the settlement of Germantown. The relations between the Mennonites of Holland and Switzerland had always been very close. Twice had the former made formal protest to Berne and Zürich in regard to the persecution of their brethren; they

resemblance between this community of scholars and the Pantisocracy dreamed of by Coleridge and Southey one hundred years later, according to which "on the banks of the Susquehanna was to be founded a brotherly community, where selfishness was to be extinguished and the virtues were to reign supreme."

[21] Kelpius died before 1709. He believed that he was to be taken up into heaven alive like Elijah, and was bitterly disappointed when he felt the approach of death, and the chariot of fire did not appear. At his funeral, the body was buried as the sun was setting, and a snow-white dove was released heavenward, while the Brethren, looking upward with uplifted hands, repeated thrice, "Gott gebe ihm eine selige Auferstehung." (See Sachse, German Pietists, p. 248.)

[22] It was Conrad Matthai, one of the last survivors of the Hermitage on the Ridge, who advised Conrad Beissel to go to the Conestoga, there to live a life of contemplation and solitude.

had subscribed large sums of money to alleviate the sufferings of the exiled Swiss in the Palatinate, and a society had been formed for the purpose of affording systematic assistance to all their suffering fellow believers. It was through them, undoubtedly, that the stream of Swiss emigration was first turned to Pennsylvania, where the success of Germantown seemed to assure a similar prosperity to all.[23]

We have seen above how widespread the Anabaptist movement had been in Switzerland, especially in the cantons of Zürich and Berne. Of all their doctrines, that of refusing to bear arms was the most obnoxious to the state, which depended on its citizens for defence in time of aggression. It must be confessed that the Swiss Mennonites were the most intractable of people. Exiled again and again, they persisted every time in returning to their native land.[24] In 1710

[23] As early as 1684 at least one of the inhabitants of Germantown was a Swiss, Joris Wertmuller from Berne; see letter from him to his brother-in-law Benedict Kuntz in Pennypacker, p. 152. In 1694 George Gottschalk came from Lindau on Lake Constance.

[24] The condition and treatment of the Mennonites in Switzerland were very much like that of the Quakers in New England. The doctrines of the two sects were the same, while the Calvinistic theocracy of Massachusetts, in its union of Church and State, closely resembled the government of Berne and Zürich. The Quakers, like the Mennonites, were fond of

the Canton of Berne itself made an effort to get rid of its troublesome sectaries by sending under escort a large number of them to Holland, hoping thence to deport them to America. This effort failed through the refusal of Holland and England to be a party to such enforced emigration.

In 1711, however, the Mennonites of Berne were offered free transportation down the Rhine, permission to sell their property, and to take their families with them—on condition, however, that they pledge themselves never to return to Switzerland. Their friends in Holland urged them to do this, and especially through the untiring efforts of the Dutch ambassador in Switzerland, Johann Ludwig Runckel, the exportation finally occurred.[25] About this very time began the settlement of Lancaster County by Swiss Mennonites, and undoubtedly many of the above were among them.[26] In the archives of Amster-

public discussion, and could not be out-argued. Both were at first treated mildly; both were exiled and insisted on returning; both were flogged, imprisoned, and finally killed. (See Fiske, Beginnings of New England, p. 187.)

[25] Cf. p. 24.

[26] The names given by Müller (pp. 307 ff.) are identical with those of the Lancaster County Swiss, among them being Gerber, Gäumann, Schürch, Galli, Haldiman, Bürki, Rohrer, Schallenberger, Oberli, Jeggli, Wisler, Hauri, Graf, Wenger,

dam we find a letter of thanks to Holland written by Martin Kündig, Hans Herr, Christian Herr, Martin Oberholtzer, Martin Meili and Jacob Müller. This letter was dated June 27, 1710, and states that they were about to start for the New World. October 23d of the same year we find a patent for ten thousand acres of land on Pequea Creek, Conestogoe (later a part of Lancaster County, which was not organized till 1729), made out in the names of Hans Herr and Martin Kündig, who acted as agents of their country-men, some of whom had already arrived, and others of whom were to come. No sooner had these first settlers become established than Martin Kündig was sent back to Germany and Switzerland to bring over those who wished to share their fortune in what was then an impenetrable forest, but is now known as the garden-spot of the United States, Lancaster County. Kündig and Herr [27] seem to have been the leaders of this

Neukomm, Flückiger, Rubeli, Rüegsegger, Krähenbühl, Huber, Bühler, Kuenzi, Stähli, Rubi, Zürcher, Bucher, Strahm. Among those exiled in 1710 were the names of Brechbühl, Baumgartner, Rupp, Fahrni, Aeschlimann, Maurer, Ebersold, and others. All these names—which, more or less changed, are common throughout the State and country to-day —are of Bernese origin. The Landis, Brubacher, Meili, Egli, Ringer, Gut, Gochnauer, and Frick families came from Zürich.

[27] Hans Herr, born in 1660, was the minister and pastor of

emigration. From 1710 on, their names frequently occur in the public land records of Pennsylvania as taking up choice bits of farming land and having them turned over to their countrymen, whose interests they represented.[28] We have such records as late as 1730, when they took up 124 acres of land for Jacob Brubaker in the present township of East Hempfield.[29]

In the next important colony of this second period the scene shifts from Lancaster to what is now Berks County. In order to understand the causes leading up to this settlement we must turn our attention for a moment to the exceedingly interesting facts connected with the early German immigration to New York. In the year 1709 a very large influx of Palatines came to England with the expectation of being aided there to cross the Atlantic. The general causes

the early Swiss settlers in Lancaster County; he had five sons, all of whom came over with him, and from whom is descended a large posterity.

[28] "Agreed with Martin Kundigg and Hans Herr of 5000 acres of land, to be taken up in severall parcells about Conestogo and Pequea Creeks at £10 p. Ct', to be paid at the Returns of the Surveys and usual quitrents, it being for settlements for severall of their Countrymen that are lately arrived here. The Warr't signed, dat. 22d 9ber. 1717." (Minute Book "H" of the Board of Property. Penn. Arch., 2d Ser., vol. XIX. p. 622.)

[29] *Ellis* and *Evans*, Hist. Lanc. Co., p. 868.

of this emigration are those discussed in Chapter I ; the immediate occasion seems to have been the special efforts made by certain agents of Queen Anne to induce emigration to her Majesty's colonies in America. The presence of so large a number of foreigners was an embarrassing problem for the government, and various plans were proposed for their distribution ; three thousand eight hundred were sent to Ireland, where many of their descendants still live;[30] others were sent to the Carolinas; and in 1709, at the suggestion of Governor Robert Hunter, about three thousand were shipped to New York, for the purpose of manufacturing ships' stores for the English Government. These settled at first on both banks of the Hudson not far from the present town of Saugerties, where they remained in a constant state of discontent until the winter of 1712–1713, when, Hunter's scheme having proved itself to be visionary, they set out for the valleys of the Schoharie and the Mohawk, which had all along been the goal of their desires, and which they reached after a two weeks' journey through the trackless wilderness, after hav-

[30] To this stock belonged Philip *E*mbury and Barbara Heck, the founders of Methodism in America. For details concerning the *I*rish Palatines see Crook, ''*I*reland and the Centenary of American Methodism.''

ing suffered greatly from hunger and cold. The descendants of these people now form a large proportion of the inhabitants of that district.[31]

We have to do here, however, only with the small number who, in consequence of difficulties in regard to the titles of their land, were forced to leave the homes which they had built with the labor of many years, and who in 1723 painfully made their way through the wilderness of northern New York to the head-waters of the Susquehanna and thence floated down that river, passing the sites of the present cities of Binghamton, Pittston, and Wilkesbarre till they arrived at the mouth of the Swatara Creek, up which they made their way to the district now known as Tulpehocken.[32] In the Colonial Records of Pennsylvania we find a petition of these settlers, thirty-three families in all, in which we

[31] For further details of this exceedingly interesting story see Kapp, O'Callaghan, and Cobb. Among the well-known men of this stock may be mentioned *Edwin* F. Uhl, *Ex*-Ambassador to Germany ; W. C. Bouck, governor of New York from 1843–45 ; and Surgeon-General Sternberg.

[32] " And that bold-hearted yeomanry, honest and true,
 Who, haters of fraud, give to labor its due,   •
 Whose fathers of old sang in concert with thine,
 On the banks of Swetara, the songs of the Rhine,—
 The German-born pilgrims who first dared to brave
 The scorn of the proud in the cause of the slave."

         (Whittier, vol. III. p. 47.)

have, in their own words, a brief sketch of the vicissitudes through which they were forced to pass in seeking a home in the New World:

" This Petition Humbly Sheweth

" That your petitioners being natives of Germany, about fifteen years agoe were by the great goodness and royal bounty of her late Majesty Queen Anne, relieved from the hardships which they then suffered in Europe and were transported into the colony of New York, where they settled. But their families increasing, and being in that Government confined to the scant allowance of ten acres of land to each family, whereon they could not well subsist. Your petitioners being informed of the kind reception which their countrymen usually met with in the Province of Pennsylvania, and hoping that they might with what substance they had acquire larger settlements in that Province, did last year leave their settlements in New York Government and came with their families into this Province," etc. [33]

The petition adds that fifty more families desired to come, if they received favorable conditions.[34]

During the whole of this second period immi-

[33] Colonial Records, vol. III. p. 341.

[34] Many of these came in 1728 and 1729 ; among those who came in the latter year was the well-known Conrad Weiser.

gration into Pennsylvania went on; the numbers, however, although far in excess of the first period, have been largely exaggerated. Reliable documents are wanting, and the statements made are usually guesswork. It has been recklessly estimated that as many as fifty thousand came before 1730. On March 16, 1731, the minutes of the Synodical Deputies of Holland state that the total baptized membership of the Reformed in Pennsylvania was thirty thousand.[35] That this could not be true we need only to refer to the figures concerning the whole population given by Proud.[36] As there was no census at that time,

[35] Rev. John B. Rieger, however, in a letter dated November 22, 1731, estimates the number at less than three thousand, which is nearer the truth, as Boehm in his report of 1734 gives the actual number of communicants as 386. (See Dotterer, Hist. Notes, p. 133.)

[36] In 1731 he gives the number of taxables at 9000 or 10,000, "at most," which, according to his method of multiplying by seven, would give not more than 70,000 at the highest computation. (Vol. ii. p. 275.) It is clear that nearly one-half of the total population could not have been German Reformed, and yet there are the documents! This only shows that the historian must use contemporary documents with as much caution as any other documents. As further examples of these reckless statements we may take the following : Mittelberger declares that, in 1754, 22,000 Germans and Swiss arrived in Philadelphia alone ; yet a few pages later he says that there were in Pennsylvania some 100,000 Europeans in all. Again, Kalm says that, in 1749, 12,000 came, and this statement, reproduced by Proud, has been repeated by all writers since. A

we can accept none of these statements as authoritative, and are reduced to making our own conclusions from the data at hand. We know that the increase up to 1710 was small, a few score at the most for every year. In 1708 Germantown was still a weak and struggling community. In 1710 came the Swiss of Lancaster County, some hundreds, possibly thousands, in number. Between that date and 1717 there seem to have been no large arrivals of Germans at Philadelphia. In this latter year a considerable number of Palatines and Swiss arrived. It was of these that John Dickenson spoke when he said: " We are daily expecting ships from London, which bring over Palatines in numbers about six or seven thousand. We had a parcel who came five years ago who purchased land about sixty miles west of Philadelphia, and proved quiet and industrious." These numbers were so great as

reference to the tables will show the number in 1749 and 1754 to have been respectively 7020 and 5141. Still another example of how such statements come to be made is seen in Gordon. On p. 187 he says that in one year from December, 1728, there were 6200 Germans and *others* imported; the natural inference being that the Germans formed a large majority; on p. 208, however, he gives the statistics of this very year, and out of the 6200 only *243* are Palatine passengers, the rest being chiefly *I*rish; by referring to the tables which I have drawn up it will be seen that the number of Germans who came in 1729 is 304.

to excite some alarm. In 1717 Governor Keith expressed the opinion that this immigration might prove dangerous, and thought that the experience of England in the time of the Anglo-Saxon invaders might be repeated. If these large numbers had been repeated every year, the sum total in 1727 would have been considerable; but I have been unable to find evidence to this effect.[37] The fears of Dickenson and Keith seem to find no repetition till 1727, when the long-continued stream of immigration began which makes up our third division. Furthermore, we are distinctly told by De Hoop Scheffer that the desire for emigration seemed to have lain dormant in Germany till 1726.[38] This authority based on documents in Holland, a country through which all German and Swiss emigrants had to pass on their way to America, would seem to be conclusive. My own opinion is that before 1727 the whole number of

[37] *I*ndeed there is evidence to show that German emigration was actually hindered at this time. In 1722 the Pensionary of Holland informed the Assembly that again a great number of families from Germany had arrived in vessels for the purpose of being transported *via E*ngland to the colonies of that kingdom, but that no preparation had been made for them, and the king had advised his ambassador to Holland that an order had been issued to forbid their entrance to his colonies. (Dotterer, Hist. Notes, p. 67.)

[38] See Penn. Mag., vol. II. pp. 117 ff.

German and Swiss colonists in Pennsylvania amounted to not more than fifteen thousand, or at most twenty thousand, including the natural increase of the first comers.

The third period, which we shall now discuss, is marked by the fact that we have an official record of all those who entered at the port of Philadelphia. We have seen that in 1717 the large influx of foreigners excited serious alarm. This alarm was excited anew with the renewal of large arrivals, and on October 14, 1727, the Provincial Council adopted a resolution to the effect that all masters of vessels importing Germans and other foreigners should prepare a list of such persons, their occupations, and place whence they came, and further that the said foreigners should sign a declaration of allegiance and subjection to the king of Great Britain, and of fidelity to the Proprietary of Pennsylvania. The first oath was taken in the court-house at Philadelphia, September 21, 1727, by 109 Palatines.

The above-mentioned lists[39] contain the names of the vessels and their captains, the port from which they last sailed, and the date of arrival in

[39] These lists are given by Rupp in his "Thirty Thousand Names," and may also be found in Penn. Archives, Second Series, vol. XVII.

Philadelphia. They also give in many cases the native country of the voyagers, not, however, with much detail, or so constantly as we could wish. From 1727 to 1734 they are all classed as Palatines; on September 12, 1734, one ship's company of 263 is composed of Schwenck-felders. In 1735 we find Palatines and Switzers, and on August 26, Switzers from Berne. After 1742 they are grouped together as foreigners simply, until 1749 (with two exceptions only). The lists for 1749 and 1754 are especially full in this respect, and under date of the arrival of each ship the fatherland of the new arrivals is given variously as Würtemberg, Erbach, Alsace, Zwei-brücken, the Palatinate, Nassau, Hanau, Darm-stadt, Basel, Mannheim, Mentz, Westphalia, Hesse, Switzerland, and, once only, Hamburg, Hannover, and Saxony. About this time we find the number of Catholics and Protestants given, owing undoubtedly to the fears excited by the French and Indian War. After 1754 practically no information of the above sort is given.

I have thought it of some interest and value to prepare a tabulated view of the annual immi-gration to Pennsylvania on the basis of these lists.[40]

[40] Sometimes the total number of passengers is given in the lists, sometimes only the males above the age of sixteen years.

Date.	Number.	Date.	Number.
1727	1240	1752	6189
1728	390	1753	5262
1729	304	1754	5141
1730	448	1755	226
1731	634	1756	157
1732	2168	1757	0
1733	1287	1758	0
1734	433	1759	0
1735	267	1760	0
1736	828	1761	90
1737	1736	1762	0
1738	3115	1763	589
1739	1663	1764	2329
1740	1131	1765	786
1741	1946	1766	589
1742	1092	1767	1077
1743	1794	1768	854
1744	1080	1769	408
1745	No lists	1770	554
1746	444	1771	951
1747	960	1772	903
1748	1944	1773	1659
1749	7020	1774	675
1750	4333	1775	225
1751	3951		
			68,872 [41]

In the latter case in order to obtain the total number of men, women, and children I have multiplied by three. By making careful computation of those cases where both data are given (amounting to over thirty thousand persons), I have found that the actual proportion of males above sixteen is somewhat more than one-third. Hence the figures given above are if anything slightly too large. This excess, however, may be allowed to stand as counterbalancing whatever immigration came into Pennsylvania by way of New York, Maryland, or elsewhere.

[41] These figures were at first computed from the data

We see from the above figures that there were periods of ebb and flood in the tide of immigration. The most important years are from 1749 to 1754, when the numbers became enormous, amounting for these six years to 31,896, nearly one-half of the total figures. As to the whole number of Germans in Pennsylvania in 1775, many and divergent estimates have been given; nearly all agree, however, in reckoning the proportion as about one-third of the total population, a proportion which seems to have kept itself unchanged down to the present day. If I were asked to give my estimate in regard to a matter concerning which authoritative data are wanting, I should reply, somewhat hesitatingly, as follows: Before 1727 let us assume the numbers to be 20,000, a liberal estimate; add to this the fig-

given by Rupp, but discovering later that he was not in all cases reliable, I have carefully revised them from the lists given in the Pennsylvania Archives. Proud (vol. II. p. 273) says that by an "exact account" of ships and passengers arriving at Philadelphia from nearly the first settlement of the province till about 1776, the number of Germans appear to be 39,000, and their natural increase great. His "account," however, cannot have been very exact, for two pages previously he declares that, during the summer of 1749, 12,000 Germans came to Philadelphia, "and in several other years near the same number of these people arrived annually." The two statements do not harmonize and tend to destroy our belief in Proud's accuracy. He may, however, in speaking of the 39,000, have in mind only the males over sixteen years.

ures above, 68,872, making a total of 88,872; this added to the score or so of thousands due to the natural increase of the two generations since the earliest settlements would bring up the grand total to about 110,000.[42]

One of the most interesting points of view from which to regard Pennsylvania in colonial days, says Mr. Fiske, is as the centre of distribution of foreign immigration, which from here as a starting-point spread out to all points South and West. The earliest arrivals of the people with whom we have to do in this book remained in Germantown, Philadelphia, or the immediate vicinity. Shortly after the beginning of the new century they began to penetrate the dense forests which then covered the present counties of Montgomery, Lancaster, and Berks. As the lands nearest to Philadelphia became gradually taken up, the settlers were forced to make their way further and further to the West. When no more lands remained on this side of the Susquehanna, the Germans crossed the river and founded the counties of York and Cumberland. Still later they

[42] These figures, which have been computed independently, agree substantially with those given by Proud, who gives the number of taxables in 1771 at between 39,000 and 40,000, which being multiplied by seven gives nearly 300,000, "one-third at least" being composed of Germans. (Vol. II. p. 275.)

spread over Northampton, Dauphin, Lehigh, Lebanon, and the other counties, while toward the end of the century the tide of colonization swept to the South and the newly opened West. One by one Monroe, Centre, Adams, and Cumberland counties were taken up. As early as 1732 a number of Pennsylvania Germans under Jost Hite made their way along the Shenandoah valley and settled Frederick, Rockingham, Shenandoah, and other counties of Virginia. In the central and western parts of North Carolina there were many communities formed by settlers from Berks and other counties in Pennsylvania. After the successful outcome of the French and Indian wars, when Ohio was thrown open to enterprising settlers, Pennsylvania Germans were among the pioneers of that region, many parts of which are still distinctly marked by the peculiarities of the parent colony. Still later they were in the van of the movement which little by little conquered the vast territory of the West, and subdued it to the purposes of civilization; such distinctively Pennsylvania German names as Hoover, Garver, Landis, Brubaker, Stauffer, Bowman, Funk, Lick, and Yerkes, scattered all over the West, tell the story of the part played by their bearers in the early part of the century in the conquest of the West.

Looking out upon this moving picture of the German pioneers, as they spread gradually over the vast territory of the New World, we are irresistibly reminded of our Alemannic ancestors in the far-off days of the Völkerwanderung.[43] In the eighteenth as in the fourth century, the German colonist entered the unbroken wilderness, clearing first the lands in the valleys and along the river-courses, then, as the population increased and land became scarcer, advancing further and further, climbing the sides of the mountains, and everywhere changing the primeval forest into fields covered with grain and dotted here and there with the rude buildings of the farmers.

[43] "Gleich dem Hinterwäldler in Amerikas Wildnissen musste der Alemanne vor tausend Jahren im Schweisse seines Angesichtes Arbeiten wie ein Lasttier, bis die Gegend wohnlich aussah." (Dändliker, vol. I. p. 92.)

Cf. also Boos: "Es war ein harter Kampf mit der Natur. Um der wachsenden Bevölkerung Nahrung zu schaffen, musste der Wald gerodet werden, und es entstand zahlreiche neue Dörfer," etc. (Geschichte der Rheinischen Städtekultur, vol. I. p. 162.)

CHAPTER III.

OVER LAND AND SEA.

THERE is no more attractive line of study than that which aims at revealing the daily struggles and trials, the manners and customs, the thoughts and feelings of our forefathers.[1] Where facts are wanting, the imagination of the poet, the dramatist, and the novelist is called in to round out the picture. It is this desire on the part of mankind to penetrate the veil of the past which makes the wonderful success of the historical novel possible.

Of course in a book like the present, the purpose of which is to give nothing but simple facts, all mere surmise and fancy must be rigorously excluded. And yet it ought certainly to be of interest to the descendants of the early Pennsylvania Germans to obtain some glimpse, however brief, of the daily life, the vicissitudes, the

[1] "In der *E*rinnerung an die alte Zeit und die grossen Beispeile der Vorfahren liegt eine unwiderstehliche Gewalt." (Ranke, quoted by Dändliker, II. 690.)

sufferings, the hopes and joys of their ancestors. Fortunately we have more or less material still preserved in the shape of letters, diaries, narratives, etc., in which many valuable details are given of the journey from the Old to the New World. Two hundred years ago travelling, whether on land or sea, was no easy matter, nor one to be lightly undertaken. The prospective emigrant must first transport himself, his family, and his goods by wagon to the nearest river.[2] This, of course, in the vast majority of cases was the Rhine, which was even more important as a great water-highway then than now.

We have a number of contemporary descriptions of such a journey down the Rhine. That of the Bernese Mennonites who were exiled in 1711 is given in detail and with great vividness by Müller in his " Bernische Täufer." They were shipped on boats at Berne and at Neuchâtel July 13th; meeting at Wangen, they descended the Aar to Lauffenburg on the Rhine, and thence floated down-stream to Basel, which they reached on the 16th. Here the exiles were rearranged on

[2] It is said of the Stauffer family that the sons dragged their mother in a wagon to the river and later from Philadelphia to their new home in Lancaster (see Brubacher Genealogy, p. 157). This story or legend seems like a far-off echo of that old by Herodotus of Cleobis and Bito.

three ships, in which they made the rest of the journey to Holland, whence many afterward came to Pennsylvania. The flotilla was under the command of George Ritter and his two sub-ordinates, Gruner and Haller. In addition each boat had a skilled helmsman, the necessary crew being formed from among the Brethren—of whom twenty declared themselves capable of steering—and two general overseers.[3]

Another interesting picture of the Rhine journey is given in the description of the party of

---

[3] I cannot forbear quoting here the graphic description given by Müller (p. 304) of the departure of this fleet, inasmuch as among the passengers were the ancestors of many prominent Pennsylvania families. "It has been frequently described," says Müller, "how the exiled Salzburger Protestants, laden with their scanty possessions, crossed the mountains of their native land, and, with tears in their eyes, looked back to the valleys of their home: it has been described how the bands of French emigrants wandered over the frontiers of their native land singing psalms. Our friends from the *E*mmenthal and the *O*berland found no sympathy among their fellow Swiss, as the towers of the Cathedral of Basel and the wooded heights of the Jura faded in the distance. Sitting on boxes and bundles, which were piled high in the middle of the boat, could be seen gray-haired men and women, old and feeble; yonder stood the young gazing in wonder at the shores as they slipped by. At times they were hopeful, at others sad, and their glances would alternate, now to the north, now to the south toward their abandoned home, which had driven them out so unfeelingly, and yet whose green hills and snow-capped mountains they cannot forget. Despite the comforts of religion, their sadness

four hundred Swiss Reformed led by Goetschi to
Pennsylvania. They left Zürich October 4, 1734.
At Basel they had to wait a week to get passes
through to Rotterdam. At that time France was
at war with Austria, and the armies of both countries were on either side of the river. This, of
course, was fraught with more or less danger to
the travellers, who literally had to sail between
two fires. They were constantly hailed and ordered to stop, were boarded, searched, forced to
open their chests, and were allowed to proceed
only after being fined, or rather robbed. All this
in addition to the numerous stoppages caused by
the various tariff-stations along the Rhine, of
which Mittelberger counts thirty-six from Heil-
bronn to Holland.[4]

As may be seen from the above, such travel
was extremely slow. The expedition from Berne,

could not be overcome, and from time to time some one would
begin to sing :

> " ' Ein Herzens Weh mir überkam
> Im Scheiden über d' Massen
> Als ich von euch mein Abschied nam
> Und dessmals müst verlassen.
> Mein Herz war bang
> Beharrlich lang :
> Es bleibt noch unvergessen
> Ob scheid ich gleich,
> Bleibt's Herz bei euch,
> Wie solt ich euch vergessen?' "

[4] Journey to Pennsylvania, p. 18.

described above, left that city July 13th and reached Utrecht August 2d. A similar expedition the year previous left Berne March 18th, and reached Nimwegen April 9th, while the Goetschi party spent a number of weeks in reaching Holland.

Another interesting account of such river-journeys is that of the Schwenckfelders in 1733 from Herrnhut, Saxony, down the Elbe to Hamburg. From Berthelsdorf to Pirna, six German miles, it took them two days by wagon. Here they embarked on two boats and began the descent of the Elbe, making very slow progress; the first day, from Pirna to Dresden, two miles;[5] the next four, the next five, then three, and so on, never making more than six or seven miles a day. Leaving Pirna April 22d, they reached Hamburg May 8th. Here they took passage for Amsterdam, thence to Rotterdam, where they finally embarked for the New World, making, of course, the usual stop at England to take on new provisions.

An ocean journey in the eighteenth century meant far more than it does now. If many people to-day look on the trip with repugnance, in spite of all the conveniences of modern steamers,

[5] Of course these are German miles; the distance from Pirna to Dresden by railroad is 10½ English miles.

what must have been the feelings of our forefathers? The whole journey was one continual
series of discomforts, suffering, disease, and
death. It is no wonder that many in despair
cursed their folly in undertaking such a journey.[6]

Most of the vessels that came to Pennsylvania
started from Rotterdam, where the emigrants
were embarked together with their goods and
provisions. What these latter were we get a
glimpse of in the various publications made at
that time for the information of intending passengers. Thus in the document published by
George I., the emigrant is told to present himself to one or more of the well-known merchants
of Frankfort, and to pay £3 each (children under
ten, half rates); i.e., £2 for transportation,[7] and
£1 for 70 pounds of peas, a measure of oatmeal,

[6] "For I can say with full truth that on six or seven ocean
vessels I have heard of few people who did not repent their
journey." (Letter of John Naas, Oct. 17, 1733, in Brumbaugh's History of the Brethren, p. 120.) Mittelberger paints
the picture in still darker colors, but he is always inclined to
exaggeration. See p. 21.

[7] The fare over changed naturally from time to time; we
may take as the two extremes the price given in the "Recueil
de Diverses pièces," etc., that is, £5 per head for man and
wife with provisions; for a child under ten the fare was 50
shillings; in 1773 it was £8 8s. per head. (See the agreement made with Captain Osborne, of the Pennsyvania Packet,
given in Penn. Mag., vol. XIII. p. 485.)

and the necessary beer; they would then be sent
in ships to Rotterdam, and thence carried to Virginia. First, however, in Holland one-half of the
fare must be paid, and additional provisions secured: 24 pounds of dried beef, 15 pounds of
cheese, 8¼ pounds of butter. They were advised
to provide themselves still more liberally with
edibles, with garden-seeds, agricultural imple-
ments, linen, bedding, table-goods, powder and
lead, furniture, earthenware, stoves, and especially money to buy " seeds, salt, horses, swine,
and fowls."

We may take this as a type of what was a full
outfit for the intending settler at that time. In
actual fact, however, the majority were far from
being so well provided; often they had to depend
on the charity of others.[8] Indeed, so great was
the destitution of those who passed through
Holland that the Mennonites of that country

[8] Thus the Schwenckfelders tell us how a wealthy Dutch
family generously gave them for ships' stores 16 loaves, 2 casks
of Hollands, 2 pots of butter, 4 casks of beer, 2 roasts, a quantity of wheaten bread and biscuit, 2 cases French brandy. It
is pleasing to add that the Schwenckfelders were not ungrate-
ful, and that this "bread cast upon the waters" returned after
many days; for in 1790, hearing that business reverses had
come upon the descendants of those who had helped their
fathers, they sent over a large sum of money. (See Heebner,
Geneal. Rec. of Schwenckfelders.)

formed a committee on " Foreign Needs," the purpose of which was to collect money for the assistance of their destitute brethren and others who were constantly arriving in Holland on their way to America.

Even in the best of cases, however, the food was likely to give out or spoil,[9] especially if the journey was unusually long. This in the days of sailing frequently happened. Sometimes the trip was made in a few weeks, while at other times as many months would pass. Thus when Muhlenberg came over they were 102 days on board. In a letter written by Caspar Wistar December 4, 1732, he says: " In the past year one ship among the others sailed about the sea 24 weeks, and of the 150 persons who were thereon, more than 100 miserably languished and died of hunger; on account of lack of food they caught rats and mice on the ship, and a mouse was sold for 30 kreuzer." [10] He mentions another ship which was 17 weeks on the voyage, during which about 60

[9] " Unser Tractament an Speis und Tranck war fast schlecht, denn 10 Personen bekamen wochendlich 3 pfund Butter, täglich 4 Kannten Biers und 1 Kanten Wassers. Alle Mittage 2 Schüsseln voll Erbsen und in der Wochen 4 Mittage Fleisch, und 3 Mittage gesalzene Fische . . . und jedesmal von dem Mittagessen so viel aufsparen muss dass man zu Nacht zu essen habe." (Pastorius, Beschreibung, p. 36.)

[10] Dotterer, Perkiomen Region, vol. II. p. 120.

persons died. Many more similar details might be given. The discomforts of the journey were many; the boats were almost always over-crowded. The Schwenckfelders relate that their ship of only 150 tons burden had over 300 persons on board. Later, in the days of speculation, overcrowding was the rule.

Often the ship had to wait days or even weeks for favorable winds or the necessary escort. Pastor Kunze, in his " Reise von England nach Amerika," tells how he came on board his vessel July 20, 1770, but it was the 6th of August before they passed Land's End; and we learn from Pastor Handschuh that, although he embarked on his ship September 25, 1747, they did not finally sail till January 14, 1748; he arrived in Philadelphia April 5.[11] Surely under such circumstances it was necessary to possess their souls in patience.

The actual sea voyage was invariably fraught with fear if not with danger, although the latter was by no means seldom. Sickness did not fail to declare itself; the mortality was often execssively high. On the vessel in which Penn came over thirty-six people died of the small-pox; this was only an earnest of the terrible harvest of death in the following years. Of the three

[11] Hall. Nachrichten, I. p. 155.

thousand who came to New York in 1709 nearly one-sixth had died on the voyage, and Sauer says that in one year more than two thousand had succumbed to hardship and disease. Indeed, later in the century when speculation had taken possession of ocean transportation, sickness was so unfailing a concomitant of the journey that ship-fever was generally known in Philadelphia as " Palatine fever." Children especially suffered, those from one to seven years rarely surviving the voyage.[12] There is a world of pathos in such simple statements as those which we find in the diary of Naas: " July 25th a little child died; the next day, about 8 o'clock, it was buried in the sea; August 7th a little child died, and in the same hour a little boy was born; August 23d again a child died, and was buried at sea that evening; on the 11th again a little child died, *without anybody having noticed it until it was nearly stiff;* the 13th a young woman died in childbirth, and was buried at sea, with three children, two of them before and now the third, the one just born, so that the husband has no one left now." [13]

The danger of shipwreck was always at hand,

[12] Mittelberger, p. 23. He says he himself saw no less than thirty-two children thus die and thrown into the sea.

[13] Brumbaugh, pp. 112 ff.

and the legend of Palatine Light still preserves the memory of a vessel of German immigrants wrecked off Block Island, with the loss of almost every one on board.[14] During nearly the whole of the eighteenth century England was at war with some one or other of her neighbors; this added, of course, to the dangers as well as the vexations of " them that went down to the sea in ships." In 1702 she joined the Grand Alliance against France; in 1740 she was at war with Spain; from 1743–1748 and from 1756–1763 with France again; while ever on the political horizon hovered the fear of the Turk.[15] During the early part of the century the American coast swarmed with pirates and added a new terror to ocean travel.[16] As soon as a strange vessel was discovered, all was excitement and

[14] See, for other examples of shipwreck, Mittelberger, pp. 34-36. Whittier has a poem on the Palatine Light.

[15] It was not mere rhetoric when the Mennonites of Germantown, in their protest to the Quakers against slavery, wrote : "How fearfull and fainthearted are many on sea when they see a strange vessel, being afraid it should be a Turck, and they should be tacken and sold for slaves in Turckey." Watson says that Pastorius was chased by Turks in 1683. (Annals, p. 61.)

[16] Fiske says that never in the world's history was piracy so thriving as in the seventeenth and the first part of the eighteenth century ; he places its golden age from 1650–1720. (Old Virginia and her Neighbors, vol. II. p. 338.)

fear on board, until it could be ascertained whether it was friend or foe. We have a vivid glimpse of this excitement at such a moment in Muhlenberg's Journal: Shortly after leaving Dover, "a two-masted vessel sailed directly toward them. The captain, stating that occasionally Spanish privateers had taken ships by pretending to be French fishing-vessels, made a display of both courage and strength, by commanding the drummer to belabor his drum, the guns to be loaded, and everything to be made ready for defensive action; then asked the foe, through the speaking-trumpet, what they wanted, and received the comforting answer that they were Frenchmen engaged in fishing." In the account given by a member of Kelpius's party in 1694, shots were actually fired by the enemy, one of which broke a bottle which the ship's boy was carrying in his hand; fortunately, however, no further damage was done. Similar scenes are frequently related in contemporary documents.[17]

In general, however, the days passed much as they do now, in alternation of storm and calm, sunshine and rain. The ordinary events of hu-

[17] Cf. Handschuh's Diarium, in Hall. Nach., I. p. 163; also Narrative of Journey of Schwenckfelders, in Penn. Mag., vol. x. pp. 167 ff.

man life went on in this little floating world, tossed about by the waves of the sea; the two poles of human existence, birth and death, were in close proximity; [18] and even amid the hardships and sadness there was still room for courtship and marriage.[19] Various means were employed to pass away the time, among those mentioned by Muhlenberg and others being boxing (by the sailors), singing worldly songs, disputations, mock-trials, etc. These were, however, the amusements chiefly of the English. In general the Germans had other means of passing the time. In practically every account we have they are shown to be deeply religious, holding divine service daily, and particularly fond of singing the grand old hymns of the Church.[20] This piety did not desert them in times of danger, as many incidents which might be quoted show. Muhlen-

[18] On almost every voyage children were born at sea.

[19] In the journey of Goetschi's party down the Rhine, he had appointed four marriage officials for his party. At Neuwied four couples went ashore to be married, among them Wirtz, who married Goetschi's daughter Anna. (Good, p. 176.)

[20] "These poor people often long for consolation, and I often entertained and comforted them with singing, praying, and exhorting; and whenever it was possible, and the winds and waves permitted it, I kept daily prayer-meetings with them on deck." (Mittelberger, p. 21. Cf. also Handschuh, in Hallesche Nachrichten, vol. I. pp. 156 ff.)

berg tells us that during the above-described excitement at the sight of what was feared might prove to be a Spanish war-vessel, he made inquiry after a certain Salzburger family on board, and was pleased to find the mother with her children engaged in singing Luther's battle-hymn, "Ein feste Burg ist unser Gott."[21] Wesley describes a similar incident which occurred during his voyage to Georgia in 1736. A terrible storm had arisen; "In the midst of the psalm wherewith their service began, the sea broke over, split the mainsail in pieces, covered the ship, and poured in between the decks, as if the great deep had already swallowed us up. A terrible screaming began among the English. The Germans calmly sang on. I asked one of them afterward, 'Was [*sic*] you not afraid?' He answered, 'I thank God, no.' I asked, 'But were not your women and children afraid?' He replied mildly, 'No; our women and children are not afraid to die.'"[22]

The earliest groups of Germans came over under the auspices of special companies or organizations, mostly religious, such as the Frankfort Company, the party of mystics under Kel-

[21] Mann, Life and Times of H. M. Mühlenberg, p. 45.
[22] John Wesley, Journal, vol. I. p. 17.

pius, the Schwenckfelders in 1733, and the Moravians in 1742; often a clergyman would personally conduct his flock across the ocean, as in the case of Goetschi. The Mennonites who came to Lancaster County in 1710 and the following years were helped by their brethren in Holland, where the Mennonites were not only tolerated, but had become wealthy and prominent. Not forgetful in their prosperity of the trials of their less fortunate brothers, they had formed a society for the aid of the Palatines and Swiss who were forced to leave their native lands; with the money thus collected they furnished the emigrants not only with passage-money to America, but with provisions, tools, seeds, etc.[23]

During the greater part of the eighteenth century, however, especially the latter half, the German and Swiss emigrants were the victims of fraud and oppression. The English ship-owners, seeing the profit of transporting the emigrants to be greater than carrying freight, employed every means to induce emigration, chief among these means being German adventurers who had themselves lived in Pennsylvania. They would

[23] See the interesting account of their services by De Hoop Scheffer, translated by Judge Pennypacker in Penn. Mag., vol. II, pp. 117 ff.

travel luxuriously throughout Germany, inducing their countrymen, by the most exaggerated
statements concerning the riches to be found in
the New World, to try their fortunes beyond the
sea. These agents, known as " Newlanders,"
were generally men of the most unscrupulous
character.

The best contemporaneous accounts of these
abuses are given by Muhlenberg, Sauer, and
Mittelberger.[24] According to the former the
Newlanders received free passage and a certain
fee for every family or single person whom they
could persuade to go to Holland, there to make
arrangements with the ship-owners for their
transportation. Muhlenberg tells how they
paraded in fine clothing, pulling out ostenta-
tiously their watches, and in general acting as
rich people do. They spoke of America as if it
were the Elysian Fields, in which the crops
grew without labor, as if the mountains were of
gold and silver, and as if the rivers ran with milk
and honey. The victims of these blandishments,

[24] Muhlenberg is the most temperate, Sauer the most indignant, and Mittelberger the most lurid. The book of the
latter must be read with a great deal of allowance. He was
evidently a disappointed man, and being forced to leave
Pennsylvania and return home, he gives a picture of the sufferings and disillusions of his countrymen in that province
which does not accord with what we learn from other sources.

on arriving in Holland, having often to wait a long
time before leaving, were frequently obliged to
borrow money from the contractors themselves,
in order to buy provisions and pay their passage. Before leaving they had to sign an agreement in English, which they did not understand.[25] "If the parents died during the passage, the captain and the Newlanders would act
as guardians of the children, take possession of
their property, and, on arrival in port, sell the
children for their own and their dead parents'
freight. On arriving at Philadelphia, the agreement signed by the emigrant in Holland, together with the total amount of money loaned,
passage and freight, is produced; those who
have money enough to pay the exorbitant demands are set free, after being examined by the
doctor, and taking the usual oath of allegiance
at the court-house. All others are sold to pay
the transportation charges."[26] So far Muhlenberg, who gives an exceedingly clear and interesting account of this nefarious system. Christopher Sauer, at that time, through his newspaper and almanac, perhaps the most influential
German in Pennsylvania, is moved to indigna-

[25] One of these agreements is published in Penn. Mag., vol.
XIII. p. 485.

[26] Hallesche Nachrichten, vol. II. pp. 459 ff., note.

tion at the state of affairs. On March 15 and
again May 12, 1755, he writes two letters to Governor Denny, remonstrating at the abuses. He
tells how the emigrants are packed like herrings,
how in consequence of improper care two thousand died in one year. "This murdering trade
made my heart ache, especially when I heard
that there was more profit by their death than
by carrying them alive." "They filled the vessels with passengers and as much of the merchants' goods as they thought fit, and left the
passengers' chests, etc., behind; and sometimes
they loaded vessels with Palatines' chests. But
the poor people depended upon their chests,
wherein was some provision such as they were
used to, as dried apples, pears, plums, mustard,
medicines, vinegar, brandy, butter, clothing,
shirts and other necessary linens, money, and
whatever they brought with them; and when
their chests were left behind, or shipped in some
other vessel, they had lack of nourishment."

Not all the victims of these unscrupulous ship-
pers were poor and of humble rank. Sauer ex-
pressly says that many had been wealthy people
in Germany, and had lost hundreds and even
thousands of pounds' worth by leaving their
chests behind, or by being robbed, "and are
obliged to live poor with grief." These state-

ments are borne out by Mittelberger, who says that people of rank, " such as nobles, learned or skilled people," when they cannot pay their passage and cannot give security are treated like ordinary poor people, and obliged to remain on board till some one buys them.[27]

But enough has been said to show how great was the abuse, and to justify the indignation of Muhlenberg and Sauer. These abuses continued long afterwards, even down to the first decade of the nineteenth century; indeed, the worst cases occur after the Revolution, and hence after the period discussed in this book. After all there is no use dwelling on such details; they were undoubtedly, to a greater or less extent, the necessary accompaniments of a great, unsupervised movement of emigration; a movement which, although it had its dark side, was nevertheless fraught with untold blessing to thousands.

The custom referred to above, of selling the

[27] Mittelberger, p. 39. He gives an example of this in the case of "a noble lady" who in 1753 came to Philadelphia with two half-grown daughters and a young son. She entrusted all her fortune to a Newlander, who robbed her ; in consequence of which both she and her daughters were compelled to serve. John Wesley in his Journal, under date March 6, 1736, tells the story of John Reinier from Vevay, Switzerland, who came to America "well provided with money, books, and drugs," but, being robbed by the captain, was forced to sell himself for seven years.

passengers to pay their charges,—a custom known as redemptionism,—was not confined to the Germans. In the previous century the custom existed among the French of the West Indies; the "engagés," as they were called, selling themselves to serve three years. Many of the Huguenots were thus disposed of.[28] The system was also in vogue in all the English colonies except New England. Fenwick, in his Proposal of 1675,—intended to draw immigration to New Jersey,—urges it as a reasonable means of coming to the New World and obtaining a plantation; Furley, Penn's agent, also urges the same thing. In Pennsylvania it was entirely respectable, and many who afterwards grew to distinction came over this way.[29] The Germans as servants seem not to have come over until well on in the eighteenth century; later, however, they became very numerous.

The condition of the redemptioners was not in general very hard. They were usually well

[28] Baird, Huguenot Emigration to America.

[29] Among them are said to have been Matthew Thornton, one of the Signers of the Declaration of Independence; the parents of General Sullivan; the wife of the famous Sir William Johnson of Mohawk Valley; and Charles Thompson, secretary of the Continental Congress (see Watson, p. 544). Gordon (p. 556) writes that many of the German and Irish settlers were of this class, "from whom have sprung some of the most reputable and wealthy inhabitants of the province."

their service received a certain outfit.[30]   Indeed, for a single man, or for children, it was often of decided advantage, being a sort of apprenticeship in which the customs of the new land were learned. It is said that some voluntarily sold themselves for the sake of the experience they would get.[31] The chief hardship was when a whole family became the victims of fraudulent merchants, and on arriving in a land of freedom, as they fondly hoped, saw themselves torn asunder, sold to different parts of the country, parents and children being thus separated for years, perhaps forever.[32]

[30] See Fenwick, Furley, Kalm, etc.

[31] Kalm, vol. I. p. 304, says: "Many of the Germans who come hither bring money enough with them to pay their passage, but rather suffer themselves to be sold, with a view that during their servitude they may get some knowledge of the language and quality of the country and the like, that they may the better be able to consider what they shall do when they have got their liberty." Cf. also: "For many young people it is very good that they cannot pay their own freight. These will sooner be provided for than those who have paid theirs, and they can have their bread with others and soon learn the ways of the country." (Letter of John Naas ; see Brumbaugh, p. 123.)

[32] See the pathetic account given by Muhlenberg, Hallesche Nachrichten, II. p. 461: "Weit und breit von einander, unter allerlei Nationen, Sprachen und Zungen zerstreuet, so dass sie selten ihre alten Eltern, oder auch die Geschwister sich einander im Leben wieder zu sehen bekommen." The story of Evangeline must have frequently repeated itself in those days.

CHAPTER IV.

MANNERS AND CUSTOMS OF THE PENNSYLVANIA-GERMAN FARMER IN THE EIGHTEENTH CENTURY.

ALTHOUGH Christopher Sauer says that many of the early Germans of Pennsylvania had been wealthy at home; although Mittelberger distinctly tells us that " persons of rank, such as nobles, learned or skilled people," were often sold as redemptioners, yet the large majority of the eighteenth century settlers were poor. This of course was through no fault of their own; the devastations of the Thirty Years' War, and especially the wanton destruction ordered by Louis XIV. in the last decade of the seventeenth century, had reduced to poverty thousands who had been prosperous farmers and tradesmen; and not for two hundred years was this prosperity fully restored to those who remained in the Fatherland.[1] Whatever property they had been able to gather together was used up in the ex-

[1] See p. 6.

penses of descending the Rhine and crossing the ocean, or was stolen by the unprincipled ship-owners and their parasites, the Newlanders.

It was not long, however, before this poverty was transformed into prosperity and plenty. This was especially true of the Mennonites, who came when the land was cheap, and who bought large quantities thereof. Later, property in the immediate neighborhood of Philadelphia and the adjacent counties became dearer and dearer, and finally not to be obtained at all. Those who came towards the middle of the century had to move further and further into the wilderness beyond the Blue Mountains or across the Susquehanna.[2] After the Revolution, however, prosperity reigned throughout the whole of the farming regions of the State.

This prosperity was not entirely due to the peculiar conditions of Pennsylvania at that time; others, both of those who came before and of those who afterwards followed the same kind of life, did not succeed.[3] It was largely due to the indomitable industry, the earnestness, the frugality,

[2] Dahero gehen sie immer weiter fort in das wilde Gebüsche, . . . und aus Noth weiter fortgehen müssen in die noch unbebauten *Einöden.*'' (Muhlenberg, Hall. Nach., I. p. 342.)

[3] Pastorius says of the Swedes and Dutch that they ''are poor economists, have neither barns nor stalls, let their grain

and the consummate agricultural skill of the Germans.[4]   When, in the Palatinate, they had been bereft of all, houses, barns, cattle, and crops, one thing they had still kept: the skill inherited from thirty generations of land-cultivators, a skill that had made the Palatinate literally the " garden-spot " of Germany.[5]

This same skill, brought to Pennsylvania, soon changed the unbroken forest to an agricultural community as rich as any in the world.   It is doubtful if ever any colony was so perfectly adapted to its settlers as Pennsylvania was to the Germans of one hundred and fifty years ago. The soil, though heavily timbered, was fertile and only needed the hand of the patient husbandman in order to blossom as the rose; when the Germans arrived this condition was fulfilled. While their English and Scotch-Irish neighbors usually followed the course of rivers or larger streams, thus lessening the labor of clearing, the Germans and Swiss would plunge boldly into an un-

lie unthreshed," etc. (Pennypacker, p. 138.) The Scotch-Irish likewise were inferior in this respect to the Germans, who soon had possession of the best farming land in the State.

[4] " The Germans seem more adapted for agriculture and the improvement of a wilderness, and the Irish for trade," etc. (Proud, II. p. 274.) Penn told Pastorius " dass ihm der Eyffer der Hoch-Teutschen im Bauen sehr wohl gefalle."

[5] So called by Schlözer one hundred and fifty years ago.

broken wilderness, often fifty or sixty miles from
the nearest habitation, knowing well that where
the heaviest forest growth was, there the soil
must be good.[6]   They could, in very truth, say
with the Swiss in Schiller's " Wilhelm Tell ":

> "Wir haben diesen Boden uns erschaffen
>   Durch unserer Hände Fleiss, den alten Wald,
>   Der sonst der Bären wilder Wohnung war,
>   Zu einem Sitz für Menschen umgewandelt." [7]

The best soil in Pennsylvania for farming purposes is limestone, and it is a singular fact that
almost every acre of this soil is in possession of
German farmers.[8]   If we may make a distinction
where all are excellent, the Mennonites may
be said to illustrate to the highest degree the
skill in agriculture; as Riehl says, " Wo der
Pflug durch goldene Auen geht da schlägt auch
der Mennonite sein Bethaus auf." [9]   It is due to
the fact that Lancaster County is especially rich
in limestone soil and is largely inhabited by Men-

[6] Penn says, "the back lands being generally three to one
richer than those that lie by navigable rivers." (Proud, I. p.
247.)

[7] Schiller, "Wilhelm Tell," II. 2.

[8] The late *Eckley* B. Coxe said not long ago that a letter from
Bethlehem written to his grandfather asserts that in Pennsylvania, if you are on limestone soil, you can open your mouth
in Pennsylvania Dutch and get a response every time. (Proceedings of Penn. Ger. Soc., vol. V. p. 102.)

[9] Die Pfälzer, p. 374.

nonites that it has become the richest farming
county in the United States.[10]

[10] This is not mere rhetoric, but a sober statement of actual
fact, as any one who will take the trouble to look up the agricultural statistics of the country may easily see. In the history
of Lancaster County by *E*llis and *E*vans we find the statement
made that " within the memory of the oldest inhabitants there
had been no entire failure of all its crops.'' Six-sevenths of
the entire area, or 463,000 acres, are farm-lands. In 1890
the value of agricultural products in Lancaster County was
$7,657,790, while St. Lawrence County, N. Y., the next
richest agricultural county had crops valued at $6,054,160, or
$1,603,630 less than Lancaster.

As an instance of the rapidity with which the new settlers
became prosperous we may take the inventory of the " goods
and chattels " of Andrew Ferree of Lancaster County, who
died in 1735, only twenty-five years after the first settlement in
that county :

" To wheat in the stack at £8—wheat and rye
    in the ground, £6...................... £14- 0-0
To great waggon, £12—little waggon, £5.... 17- 0-0
To a plow and two pairs of irons........... 1-10-0
To two mauls and three iron wedges, 9s.—to
    four old weeding hoes, 4s. 13-0
To a spade and shovel, 8s.—to a matock and
    three dung forks, 10s................. 18-0
To two broad-axes, 12s.—to joyner's axe and
    adze, 7s........................... 19-0
To sundry carpenter tools, £1—sundry joiner's
    tools, £2-5s.... .... 3- 5-0
To seven duch sythes [*sic*]................ 12-0
To four stock bands, two pair hinges, sundry
    old iron........................... 14-0
To a hand-saw, £2—to five sickles and two old
    hooks 11-0

It is surprising how rapidly agriculture prospered in Pennsylvania. In a letter on Braddock's campaign, written by William Johnston, September 23, 1755, we find the following remarks: " Pennsylvania is much the best country of any I have seen since I have been upon the continent, and much more plenty of provisions

To a cutting-box, two knives, £1—to twenty-baggs, £2–10s.	3–10–0
To two pair chains, 14s.—two hackles, £1–10 —to five bells, 12s	2–16–0
To four smal chains and other horse geers at..	1– 4–0
To other horse geers at £1–10s.—to a man's saddle at £1–10.	3– 0–0
To three falling axes at 10s.—to two fowling pieces, £2	2–10–0
To a large Byble	2– 0–0
To two fether beds at £6—to wearing cloaths, £7	13– 0–0
To sundry pewter, £2–8—to a box iron, 4s.	2–12–0
To sundry iron ware, £2—to a watering pot, 6s.	2– 6–0
To sundry wooden ware at £1—to two iron pot-racks, £1	2– 0–0
To four working horses, £24—to a mare and two colts, £11.	35– 0–0
To six grown cows at £15—to ten head of young cattle, £13–10	28–10–0
To eleven sheep, £3–17—to swine, £1–10.	5– 7–0
To two chests, 15s.—to a spinning-wheel, 8s..	1– 3–0
To sley, 6s.—to cash.	2– 8–0
To cash received for a servant girle's time....	3– 0–0
	£152– 8-6 "

than Maryland or Virginia." [11] Of Lancaster, the county town, Johnston says: " You will not see many inland towns in England so large as this, and none so regular; and yet this town, I am told, is not above twenty-five years' standing,[12] and a most delightful country round it. It is mostly inhabited by Dutch people."

That this prosperity was largely due to the Germans is acknowledged by the English themselves. Thus Governor Thomas says in 1738: " This province has been for some years the asylum of the distressed Protestants of the Palatinate and other parts of Germany, and I believe it may truthfully be said that the present flourishing condition of it is in great measure owing to the industry of these people." [13] We have an interesting glimpse of the skill with which these

[11] Penn. Mag., vol. XI. pp. 93 ff. It will be remembered that Pennsylvania was the youngest of all the colonies except Georgia, although at the time of the Revolution it was second in population.

[12] Lancaster was laid out by James Hamilton in 1730.

[13] In the preamble of the act passed by the General Assembly of Pennsylvania in 1787 to incorporate a college in Lancaster are the words : " Whereas, the citizens of this State of German birth or extraction have eminently contributed by their industry, economy, and public virtues to raise the State to its present happiness and prosperity," etc. In recent times Bancroft has said that neither the Pennsylvania Germans nor others claim for them the credit due them.

farms were worked in the description of a trip made by Governor Thomas Pownall in 1754. He visited Lancaster, " a pretty considerable town, encreasing fast and growing rich," and then goes on to say: " I saw some of the finest farms one can conceive, and in the highest state of culture, particularly one that was the estate of a Switzer. Here it was I first saw the method of watering a whole range of pastures and meadows on a hillside, by little troughs cut in the side of the hill, along which the water from springs was conducted, so as that when the outlets of these troughs were stopped at the end the water ran over the sides and watered all the ground between that and the other trough next below it. I dare say this method may be in use in England. I never saw it there, but saw it here first." [14]

It is no wonder that, in view of such extraordinary prosperity on the part of many who a short time before had been destitute exiles from their native land, Benjamin Rush exclaims: " If it were possible to determine the amount of all the property brought into Pennsylvania by the present German inhabitants of the State and their an-

[14] Penn. Mag., vol. XVIII. p. 215. This same skill in agriculture is seen likewise in the German settlements in New York, Maryland, Virginia, and even *I*reland.

cestors, and then compare it with the present amount of their property, the contrast would form such a monument of human industry and economy as has seldom been contemplated in any age or country." [15]   " How different," he goes on to say, " is their situation here from what it was in Germany! Could the subjects of the princes of Germany, who now groan away their lives in slavery and unprofitable labor, view from an eminence in the month of June the German settlements of Strasburg or Mannheim in Lancaster County, or of Lebanon in Dauphin County, or of Bethlehem in Northampton County,—could they be accompanied on this eminence by a venerable German farmer and be told by him that many of these extensive fields of grain, full-fed herds, luxurious meadows, orchards promising loads of fruit, together with the spacious barns and commodious stone dwelling-houses which compose the prospects which have been mentioned, were all the product of a single family and of one generation, and were all secured to the owners of them by certain laws, I am persuaded that no chains would be able to deter them from sharing in the freedom of their

[15] Manners of the German *I*nhabitants of Pennsylvania, p. 55.

Pennsylvania friends and former fellow subjects." [16]

Dr. Rush himself gives us many valuable hints
as to the methods by which such striking results
were obtained. His little pamphlet on "The Manners of the German Inhabitants of Pennsylvania,"
written in 1789, is the most valuable of all the
eighteenth-century sources which throw light on
the subject we are discussing. He gives many details as to the thoroughness, far-sightedness, and
attention to little things which marked the German methods of farming. Thus at the very outset, while the Scotch-Irish or English farmer
would girdle or belt the trees, and leave them to
rot in the ground, their more far-sighted neighbors would cut them down and burn them, the
underwood and bushes being grubbed out of the
ground.[17]   By this means a field was as fit for
cultivation the second year after it was cleared

[16] For further glimpses of this prosperity see the Travels of
Weld (1795) and Saxe-Weimar (1825). An interesting detail
in this connection is the appellation "King" applied to a rich
landed proprietor. An old "Dutchman" once said, speaking
of a friend, "The people call me the king of the manor [town-
ship], and they call him the king of the Octorara." In the
MS. genealogy of the Herr family, one sheet is marked
"King" Herr.

[17]   "Und hatten manchen sauren Tag, den Wald
              Mit weitverschlungenen Wurzeln auszuroden."
                        (Schiller, "Wilhelm Tell," II. 2.)

as it was twenty years afterwards. They contended that the expense of repairing a plough, which by the other method was often broken, was greater than the extra expense of grubbing the field in clearing. Their foresight and carefulness were also shown in their treatment of horses and cattle. However economical they might be with themselves, they were never so towards their live stock. These were so well fed that the horses "performed twice the labor of those horses, and the cattle yielded twice the quantity of milk of those cows, that are less plentifully fed." The Pennsylvania German's horses were well known all over the State. Indeed, says Rush, "the horse seems to feel with his lord the pleasure and pride of his extraordinary size and fat."[18] Not only were the horses well fed, but they were kept warm in winter and spared all unnecessary labor, such as dragging heavy loads of wood for winter fires, or driving about the country for mere pleasure. In this way they were able to perform prodigious feats of strength when the

[18] This love for animals is an inherited trait; cf. Freytag, "Die grösste Freude des Landmanns war die Zucht seiner Rosse." (I. p. 307.) Meyer (Deutsche Volkskunde, p. 212) repeats a proverb still current near Heidelberg which in another form is applied to the Pennsylvania farmer: "Weiber sterbe isch ka Verderbe! Aber Gäulverrecke, des isch e Schrecke."

time came, dragging the immense loads of produce over rough roads to Philadelphia, sixty
miles or more away.

The farmer's first care after getting his field
well cleared was to build an immense barn, in
which no expense was spared to make it comfortable and ample.   This was invariably done
before any thought was taken of building a
permanent home for himself.   These great
" Swisser " barns, as they are called,[19] are down
to the present day one of the characteristic features of the landscape in the eastern counties of
Pennsylvania, and have often attracted the attention of travellers, not only in the past,[20] but in
these days of railroads, when the traveller is
whirled through Lancaster and other counties
on his way to the West.   A detailed description
of them may not be out of place here.   " They
are two stories high, with pitched roof, sufficiently large and strong to enable heavy farm-
teams to drive into the upper story, to load or
unload grain.   During the first period they were
built mostly of logs, afterwards of stone, frame,

[19] Either on account of the châlet-like projection of the
upper stories, or because many of the farmers were Swiss.

[20] The Duke of Saxe-Weimar says he was particularly
struck with these barns, many of them looking like large
churches.   (Travels, vol. II. pp. 175 and 177.)

or brick, from 60 to 120 feet long, and from 50 to 60 feet wide, the lower story, containing the stables, with feeding-passages opening on the front. The upper story was made to project 8 or 10 feet over the lower in front, or with a fore-bay attached, to shelter the entries to the stables and passageways. It contained the threshing-floors, mows, and lofts for the storing of hay and grain. The most complete barns of the present day have in addition a granary on the upper floor, a celler under the driving-way, a wagon-shed, with corn-crib and horse-power shed attached." [21]

The houses at first were temporary structures built of logs. The preparation for the permanent dwelling was the business of a number of years, before the actual building operations were begun. Stones had to be quarried, lumber sawed and allowed to season; frequently two generations

[21] *Ellis* and *Evans*, Hist. Lanc. Co., p. 348. This same architectural pride of the farmer may be seen likewise in the Palatinate to-day; cf. Riehl, "Seine Oekonomiegebäude legt der reiche Gutsbesitzer mit einer fast monumentalen Schön-heit und Dauerhaftigkeit an und schmückt seinen Garten lieber als den Kirchhof." (Pfälzer, p. 155.) *E*lsewhere he calls the stables "wahre Prachthallen, massiv aus Stein, mit Pfeilern und Kreuzgewölben." (*I*bid., p. 190.) Cf. also Meyer (Deutsche Volkskunde, p. 33): "Förmliche *E*hrfurcht empfindet man in Bayern vor einem stattlichen Einzelhof: 'Vor einer Ainet (Einödhof) soll man den Hut herabthun.'"

assisted in erecting the family homestead. " These houses were generally built of stone (some of them with dressed corners), two stories high, with pitched roof and with cornices run across the gables and around the first story. A large chimney in the middle, if modelled after the German pattern, or with a chimney at either gable-end, if built after the English or Scotch idea. Many were imposing structures having arched cellars underneath, spacious hallways with easy stairs, open fireplaces in most of the rooms, oak-panelled partitions, and windows hung in weights." [22]

One of the most interesting features of these old stone houses are the quaint inscriptions which adorn most of them, usually high up on the gable wall.[23] Many inscriptions consist simply of the initials or names of man and wife, with the

[22] Weld, in 1795, says the houses were mostly built of stone and as good as those usually met with on an arable farm of 50 acres in a well-cultivated part of England. (Travels, p. 115.) For pictures and descriptions of some of these old houses see Croll, Ancient and Historic Landmarks in the Lebanon Valley.

[23] This was a common custom in the Palatinate; the religious sentiments expressed are only seen on Protestant houses, and, significantly enough, date chiefly from the years of trial in the seventeenth and eighteenth centuries. One of the earliest of such inscriptions was made by the wife of the Count Palatine Johann Kasimir of Zweibrücken, over the portal of the Castle

date of building. Others, however, are proverbs
or quotations from Bible and hymn-book, and
thus throw a good deal of light on the practical
and pious character of the builders. Thus on
the Weidman house in Clay Township, Lancaster County, are the following words:

"Wer will bauen an die Strassen
Muss ein jeder reden lassen." [24]

On Peter Bricker's house, in West Cocalico
Township, in Lancaster County, built of sand-
stone in 1759 and still as good as new, are written these words:

"Gott gesegne dieses Haus,
Und alle was da gehet ein und aus;
Gott gesegne alle sampt,
Und dazu das ganze Land."

Still more pious is the inscription on a log-house
in Albany Township, Berks County, built by
Cornelius Frees in 1743. On a large iron plate

Katharinenburg, consisting of her initials, the year (1622),
and beneath, "Wer Gott vertraut, hat wohl gebaut." (Riehl,
Die Pfälzer, p. 198.) In Switzerland, also, such inscriptions
were common, as we may see from Schiller's "Wilhelm Tell"
(1. 2), where, speaking of Stauffer's house, he says:

"Mit bunten Wappenschildern ist's bemalt,
Und weisen Sprüchen, die der Wandersmann
Verweilend liest und ihren Sinn bewundert."

[24] Riehl (Die Familie, p. 199) gives the following variation
of this verse:

"Wer da bauet an Markt und Strassen,
Muss Neider und Narren reden lassen."

which had been walled in on the side of the building are the following lines:

"Was nicht zu Gottes Ehr'
Aus Glauben geht ist Sünde;
Merck auf, O theures Hertz,
Verliere keine Stunde.
Die überkluge Welt
Versteht doch keine Waaren,
Sie sucht und findet Koth
Und läst die Perle fahren." [25]

Next to barn and dwelling-house the most important architectural product of the Pennsylvania Germans is the great Conestoga wagon, which Rush called the "ship of inland commerce." Before the advent of railroads these were the chief means of transport between the farms and towns of Pennsylvania. In them the wheat, vegetables, fruit, and, alas! whiskey,—which often formed a side industry of many a farmer,— were carried for miles to Philadelphia. Says Rush: "In this wagon, drawn by four or five horses of a peculiar breed, they convey to market, over the roughest roads, 2000 and 3000 pounds' weight of the produce of their farms. In the months of September and October it is no uncommon thing on the Lancaster and Reading roads to meet in one day fifty or one hundred of these wagons on their way to Philadelphia,

[25] Montgomery, Hist. of Berks Co.

most of which belong to German farmers." These teams were stately objects in those times; owner and driver alike took pride in them and kept them neat and trim. They consisted of five or six heavy horses, well fed and curried, wearing good harness, and sometimes adorned with bows of bells, fitted so as to form an arch above the collar. These bells were carefully selected to harmonize or chime, from the small treble of the leaders to the larger bass upon the wheel-horses. The wagon-body was necessarily built stanch and strong, but by no means clumsy. Upon them the wheelwright and blacksmith expended their utmost skill and good taste, and oftentimes produced masterpieces of work, both in shape and durability. The running-gear was invariably painted red, and the body blue. The cover was of stout white linen or hempen material, drawn tightly over, shapely, fitted to the body, lower near the middle and projecting like a bonnet in front and at the back, the whole having a graceful and sightly outline.[26]

In addition to the labor in the fields and the larger interests of the farm, the cultivation of the garden, which was the invariable adjunct of each

[26] *Ellis* and *Evans*, Hist. Lancaster Co., p. 350. The railroads put an end to these wagons. They reappeared latter in the well-known "prairie schooners."

house, was of no small importance. A love for flowers has always been the characteristic of the natives of the Palatinate,[27] and this love is quite as noticeable in Pennsylvania as in the home-country; at the present day there is not a farm-house in the country, or even a small dwelling in town, that is not adorned with flowers of many kinds, often rare. They form the one bright touch of poetry in the otherwise hard routine of farm-life.[28]

More important, however, from a practical point of view, was the cultivation of garden vegetables, in which the Germans soon reached the foremost rank; Rush says definitely that " Pennsylvania is indebted to the Germans for the principal part of her knowledge in horticulture." [29] " Since the settlement," he says, " of a number of German gardeners in the neighborhood of Philadelphia, the tables of all classes of citizens

[27] "Im übrigen Rheinland erfreut sich wohl auch der gemeine Mann am Blumenschmuck seines Hauses, aber so allgemein wie auf dem linken Ufer der Pfalz nirgends." (Riehl, Pfälzer, p. 192.) Riehl traces this love for flowers back to the days of Roman occupation of the Rhine.

[28] See Ritter's History of the Moravian Church in Philadelphia, for description of the garden of the parsonage; in addition to peach, pear, and plum trees there were various kinds of roses, lilacs, heart's-ease, lilies, etc.

[29] Rush, p. 23.

have been covered with a variety of vegetables in every season of the year."

Farming in those days was a profession and a hard and laborious one, although one sure of profitable returns. The whole life of the farmer, his labor, his thoughts, his hopes and fears, revolved about this one thing.[30] Industry was the highest virtue, idleness and sin went hand in hand.[31] "When a young man," says Rush, "asks the consent of his father to marry a girl of his choice, the latter does not so much inquire whether she be rich or poor, but whether she is industrious and acquainted with the duties of a good housewife." [32]

Even the superstitions of the early Pennsylvania Germans largely clustered about their agricultural life. In the last century, and in some

[30] It is interesting to see how many of their proverbs had to do with farming life :

"Im kleinsten Raum pflanz einen Baum
Und pflege sein, er bringt dir's ein ";

"Eine gute Kuh sucht man im Stalle"; "Gut gewetzt ist halb gemäht"; "Ein kleines Schaf ist gleich geschoren"; "Futter macht die Gäule," etc.

[31]
"Arbeite treu und glaub es fest
Dass Faulheit ärger ist als Pest,
Der Müssiggang viel Böses lehrt,
Und alle Art von Sünden mehrt.'

[32] Hence the proverb, "Eine fleissige Hausfrau ist die beste Sparbüchse.'

places well on in the nineteenth, they had many strange beliefs and curious practices. These superstitions which they brought from the Fatherland run back their roots to the early twilight of German history. It seems to be another phase of that deep touch of poetry so characteristic of German character and which has so powerfully influenced the pietistic movement in more recent times. Many of the customs of the eighteenth century, both in Germany and Pennsylvania, are survivals of heathen customs that have come floating down the centuries, the flotsam and jetsam of the religious beliefs of our pagan ancestors.

One of the most widely spread of these beliefs is the influence of the heavenly bodies. When Shakespeare makes Cassius say,

"The fault, dear Brutus, lies not in our stars,
But in ourselves, that we are underlings,"

he alludes to a belief that was well-nigh universal in the Middle Ages, that the peculiar juxtaposition of the stars and planets at the birth of any individual will have a lasting influence on the life of the new-born child. Among the Pennsylvania Germans the signs of the heavens were always noted and recorded at the birth of the child,[33] and we are told that the hermits on the

[33] This was an old German custom. Goethe begins his

Wissahickon partly gained their living by the casting of horoscopes. In the old German almanacs certain days were marked as lucky or unlucky;[34] any one born on these days was doomed to poverty; engagements or marriages contracted then were sure to be failures, and the wise man would begin no legal or other kind of business. On Ascension-day there should be no letting of blood.[35] Of especial interest to farmers was a knowledge of the times and seasons. The different phases of the moon had to be carefully observed from the almanac, for all cereals planted in the waxing of the moon grew more rapidly than in the waning. Things planted when the

"Wahrheit und Dichtung" with these words: "Am 28. August 1749, Mittags mit dem Glockenschlage zwölf, kam ich in Frankfurt am Main auf die Welt. Die Constellation war glücklich: Die Sonne stand im Zeichen der Jungfrau, und culminirte für den Tag," etc.

[34] These were Jan. 1, 2, 3, 4, 6, 11, 12; Feb. 1, 17, 18; March 14, 16; April 10, 17, 18; May 7, 8; June 17; July 17, 21; Aug. 20, 21; Sept. 10, 18; Oct. 6; Nov. 6, 10; Dec. 6, 10, 15. (See Owen, Folk-Lore from Buffalo Valley, Pa., Journal of American Folk-Lore Society, vol. IV.)

[35] The custom of blood-letting, universal throughout the middle ages, was still in full sway in Pennsylvania a hundred years ago. In the Journal of Christopher Marshall, under the date May 13, 1780 (at Lancaster) we find this entry: "This was a remarkable day for the German men and women, bleeding at (Dr.) Chrisley Neff's. So many came that I presume he must work hard to bleed the whole. Strange infatuation." (Papers of Lanc. Co. Hist. Soc., vol. III. p. 156.)

moon was in the sign of the Twins would be abundant. When the horns of the moon were down onions must be planted; beans, and early potatoes, however, when the horns were up. Apples should be picked in the dark of the moon, else they would rot. Hogs should be slaughtered during the waxing of the moon, otherwise the meat would shrink and be poor. Even the thatching of houses should be done when the horns of the moon were down, or the shingles would curl; and when fences were built, the first or lower rail should be laid when the horns were up, while the stakes should be put in and the fence finished when the horns were down. Such are a few of the affairs of life which were supposed to be done literally " by the book." [36]

Omens were frequent. It was a sign of death if a bird entered the room, if a horse neighed or dog barked at night, or if a looking-glass were broken; the same thing was supposed to be true of dreaming of having teeth pulled, or of seeing some one dressed in black.

As water was one of the most important things for every house, it is not surprising that super-

[36] This view of the influence of the moon's phases is as old as German history itself: "Aus demselben Grund, aus welchem weise Frauen zu Ariovist's Zeit den Germanen geboten, dass sie nicht vor Neumond die Schlacht beginnen sollten," etc. (Riehl, Kulturstudien, p. 47.)

natural means were employed to discover it. The following device of "smelling" for water was once common: "Hold a forked willow or peach limb with the prongs down, and move over the spot where water is desired. If water is present, the stick will turn down in spite of all you can do; it has been known to twist off the bark. The depth of water may be known by the number and strength of the dips made. Ore can be found the same way."

Also curious in their way were the weather signs. If the ears of corn burst, a mild winter will follow; but it will be cold if they are plump. If the spleen of a hog be short and thick, the winter will be short, and *vice versa*. If on February 2d the ground-hog comes out and sees his shadow, he will retire to his hole and six weeks of cold weather will follow. So, when the snow is on the ground, if turkeys go to the field or the guinea-hens halloo, there will be a thaw. If cocks crow at 10 P.M., it will rain before morning.

Witches were believed in to a more or less extent, and not only human beings, but cattle, inanimate objects, and even operations such as butter-making, were more or less subject to their malign influence. Horseshoes or broomsticks laid across the door were supposed to keep them out. Silver bullets shot at a picture of a supposed witch would bring about his or her death.[37]

The use of amulets and incantations was more or less common. By means of the former it was believed that one could make himself "kugel-fest," i.e., proof against bullets.[38] As was natural when doctors were few and far between, superstition was largely predominant in medicine. Especially were old women endowed with curative powers. Those who were born on Sunday were supposed to have power to cure headache. Among the strange methods of healing may be mentioned the following: To remove warts cut an apple, a turnip, or an onion into halves and rub the wart with the pieces and then bury them under the eaves of the house. A buckwheat cake placed on the head will remove pain; and breathing the breath of a fish will cure whooping cough. To cure "falling away" in a child make a bag of new muslin, fill with new things of any

[37] There was, however, none of the fanatic cruelty once so prevalent in Germany and which has given to Salem, Mass., such a baleful notoriety in American history.

[38] This superstition was once wide-spread in Germany; Luther believed in it firmly. See Freytag, vol. III. p. 73: "Der Glaube, dass man den Leib gegen das Geschoss der Feinde verfesten . . . könne, ist älter als das geschichtliche Leben der germanischen Völker." It was said of Captain Wetterholt, in the French and Indian War, that he was "kugel-fest."

kind, and place it on the breast of the child, letting it remain there nine days. In the meanwhile feed the child only with the milk of a young heifer. After nine days carry the bag by the little finger to a brook that flows towards the west and throw it over the shoulder. As the contents of the bag waste away the child will recover. Perhaps one of the strangest and yet most interesting of all these quaint customs was that of powwowing, or the use of magic formulas for the cure of certain diseases. It is very interesting to see this survival down to a short time ago in our own country, and still flourishing in certain parts of Germany, of a custom which is as old as the German language itself. Some of the earliest remains of Old High German and Old Saxon poetry are the so-called " Segensformen," not very different from powwowing.[39] The latter was once believed in by many of the Pennsylvania Germans. It was supposed to be especially efficacious in nose-bleed or blood-flow; in removing pain from cuts, bruises, burns; and also in skin-diseases. Thus the goitre was cured by looking at the waxing moon, passing the hand over the diseased part, and saying, "What I see must increase, what I feel must decrease." [40]

[39] Cf. Braune, Althochdeutsches Lesebuch, p. 81.
[40] Cf. Meyer, Deutsche Volkskunde, p. 116: "Hat es [a

Still more curious is the cure for snake-bite, described by Dr. W. J. Hoffman as formerly existing in Lehigh County. The following words were recited:

"Gott hot alles arschaffen und alles war gut ;
Als du alle [alter] Schlang, bisht ferflucht,
Ferflucht solsht du sei' und dei' Gift."

The speaker then with the index-finger made the sign of the cross three times over the wound, each time pronouncing the onomatope *tsing*.[41]

Even in religion these superstitions had their place, and the opening of the Bible at random and taking the verse which fell under the finger as the direct word of God—a custom which, more or less changed, has lasted for nearly fifteen hundred years [42]—was once employed by the Moravians in all the affairs of life, including marriage,

child] ein Muttermal, so blickt die Mutter, das Kind im Arm, auf einem Kreuzweg in den zunehmenden Mond und spricht, indem sie das Mal mit der Hand bestreicht : Alles, was ich sehe, nimmt zu, Alles, was ich streiche, nimmt ab."

[41] Proceedings of Penn. Ger. Society, vol. v. p. 78.

[42] "Der uralte Aberglaube, welcher schon im Jahre 506 auf dem Concilium von Agde den Christen verboten wurde, kam wieder in Aufnahme ; man schlug die Bibel oder das Gesangbuch auf, um aus zufälligem Wortlaut die Entscheidung bei innerer Unsicherheit zu finden,—der Spruch, auf welchen der rechte Daumen traf, war der bedeutsame ; ein Brauch, der noch heute fest in unserm Volke haftet, und von den Gegnern [he is speaking of the "Stillen im Lande"] schon um 1700 als 'Däumeln' verhöhnt wurde." (Freytag, vol. IV. p. 18.)

and is actually used to-day by the Mennonites in choosing their bishops.

The life of the Pennsylvania farmer was one of unremitting toil; few recreations came to break the monotony. Up before sunrise and to bed soon after sunset, such was the ordinary routine, day after day, year after year. Later in the century came more and more the usual rural festivities, quilting and husking parties, country fairs, markets, and *vendus*. Very common were the butcherings—when the friends of the family would help in the killing of hogs and the preparation of the many kinds of sausages; and especially common were the " frolics " in which the various kinds of fruit-butters, of which the Pennsylvania Germans were so fond, were boiled in huge kettles, tended to and stirred by friends and neighbors invited for the purpose.[43]

In general, however, life was uneventful, " one common round of daily task." The three great events in all lives—birth, marriage, and death—were the occasion of more or less celebration, the weddings and funerals being attended by large concourses of people, who came in wagons from far and near. The custom of providing food for

[43] Cf. Riehl (Pfälzer, p. 267) for a description of a similar combination of business and pleasure in the preparation of *Obstlatwerge* in the Palatinate.

visitors, due at first to the long distance many had
to come, soon grew to be conventional and too
often excessive. Muhlenberg frequently com-
plains of this excess at both weddings and
funerals.

An interesting description of one of these
funerals is given by Mittelberger: " In this manner such an invitation to a funeral is made
known more than fifty English miles around in
twenty-four hours. If it is possible, one or more
persons from each house appear on horseback at
the appointed time to attend the funeral. While
the people are coming in, good cake cut into
pieces is handed around on a large tin platter to
those present; each person receives then, in a
goblet, a hot West India rum punch, into which
lemon, sugar, and juniper-berries are put, which
give it a delicious taste. After this, hot and
sweetened cider is served. . . . When the people have nearly all assembled and the time for
the burial is come, the dead body is carried to
the general burial-place, or, where that is too
far away, the deceased is buried in his own
field.[44] The assembled people ride all in silence

[44] Many of these old private graveyards are now utterly
neglected and overgrown with weeds ; Riehl's description of
the neglected graveyards in the Palatinate is almost word for
word true of many in Pennsylvania : "*Eine verwilderte Hecke*

and sometimes one can count from one hundred
to five hundred persons on horseback. The
coffins are all made of fine walnut wood and
stained brown with a shining varnish." [45]

It must not be inferred from the above references to rum and cider that the Pennsylvania
Germans as a people were especially addicted to
strong drink. One hundred years ago every one
drank; in New England the settlers "were a
beer-drinking and ale-drinking race—as Shakespeare said, they were 'potent in potting';" [46] and
no public ceremony, civil or religious, occurred
in which great quantities of liquor were not
drunk. [47] The custom of drinking at funerals,

umzäunt sie. Regellose mit Gras und Gestrüpp verwachsene
Erhöhungen zeigen die Gräber an." (Pfälzer, p. 407.) He
attributes this neglect to the traditional dislike of the Reformed
people to all pomp and ceremony even in death; it is still more
true of the Mennonites, who seek the utmost simplicity in all
things temporal or spiritual,—in life and death. "Ein Mit-
glied der Gemeinschaft im Berner Jura äusserte mir gelegen-
tlich die Ansicht, man sollte nicht genötigt sein, die Toten auf
den Friedhöfen zu beerdigen ; ein jeder sollte dies auf seinem
Grundbesitz thun dürfen." (Müller, p. 62.)

[45] In making these coffins the carpenter was careful to gather
up all the shavings and sawdust and place them in the coffin,
for if any portion thereof should be brought into a house,
death was sure to follow.

[46] Alice Morse Earle, Customs and Fashions in Old New
England, p. 163.

[47] In the record of the ordination of Rev. Joseph McKean,

which Muhlenberg reprehends so stoutly, was
equally observed by the Scotch-Irish and the
the Puritans of New England.[48] Indeed we have
the authority of Benjamin Rush, who has been

in Beverly, Mass., in 1785, these items are found in the tavern-
keeper's bill:

30 Bowles of Punch before the people went to meeting	£3
80 people eating in the morning at 16d	6
10 bottles of wine before they went to meeting	1 10
68 dinners at 3s	10 4
44 bowles of punch while at dinner	4 8
18 bottles of wine	2 14
8 bowles of brandy	1 2
cherry Rum	1 10
6 people drank tea	— — 9d.

[48] Mrs. Earle gives the following bill for the mortuary ex-
penses of David Porter of Hartford, who was drowned in 1678:

By a pint of liquor for those who dived for him	£0 1s.
By a quart of liquor for those who bro't him home	2
By two quarts of wine & 1 gallon of cyder to jury of inquest	5
By 8 gallons & 3 qts. wine for funeral	£1 15
By barrel cyder for funeral	16
1 coffin	12
Windeing sheet	18

With this we may compare the bill for the double funeral-
feast of Johannes Gumre and his wife of Germantown, in
1738:

Bread & Cakes at sd Burialls	£1 1 0
Gamons Cheese & Butter	15 2
Molasses & Sugar	1 14 3

called the father of the Temperance movement in the United States, that the Pennsylvania Germans were not addicted to drunkenness.[49]

In this chapter we have endeavored to give a brief sketch of the Pennsylvania farmer a hundred years ago. It would be of some value to go more into detail concerning the routine of daily life. The limits of this book, however, will not permit this, nor perhaps would these details offer the same interest as those which tell of elegant mansions, stately equipages, and all the pomp and circumstance of colonial Virginia and New England. The houses of the simple folk whom we are discussing, their furniture, clothing,[50] food,[51] and all the accessories of life were marked by plainness and comfort rather than by elegance. Hard work, good health, an easy conscience, independence begotten of possession of a comfortable home, and land enough to provide

[49] This notwithstanding the fact that hard drinking has ever been and is to-day a national failing of the Germans. The deep religious movement in Pennsylvania one hundred years ago tended to keep the people moderate in drinking.

[50] This was at first homespun and very simple. The Moravians, Mennonites, Amish, and Ephrata Brethren had a special garb.

[51] Typical Pennsylvania-German dishes are Sauerkraut, Nudels, Schnitz und Knep, many kinds of sausages, "fruit-butters," "Fasnachts" (a kind of cruller), coldslaw, Schmier-käs, etc.

ground of modern comforts and conveniences.

CHAPTER V.

LANGUAGE, LITERATURE, AND EDUCATION.

AMONG the many interesting phenomena connected with the Pennsylvania Germans none is more striking than their persistence in clinging to their dialect. Here we have a group of people living in the very heart of the United States, surrounded on all sides by English-speaking people, almost every family having some of its branches thoroughly mixed by intermarriage with these people, yet still after the lapse of nearly two hundred years retaining to a considerable degree the language of their ancestors. Even in large and flourishing cities like Allentown, Reading, and Bethlehem much of the intercourse in business and home-life is carried on in this patois. This persistence of language is one of the strongest evidences of the conservative spirit so characteristic of the Pennsylvania-German farmer.

This love for their language, which to-day may be regarded as a really striking phenomenon, was only natural one hundred and fifty years ago.

The country was then new, the Germans formed a compact mass by themselves, the means of communication with their English neighbors were rare; it would have been surprising if they had not clung to the language of their fathers. It was precisely this same love for the mother tongue which led the Puritans to leave Holland, where they were in many respects comfortable enough.[1]

And yet this very natural desire was regarded by some at least as evidence of a stubborn and ignorant nature.[2] The very efforts made by the English—the motives of many of whom were more or less mixed—to do away with the use of

[1] "They wished to preserve their English speech and English traditions," etc. (Fiske, Beginnings of New England, p. 74.) Winslow (in his Brief Narrative, quoted by Palfrey, Hist. of N. Eng. I. p. 147) says the Puritans did not like to think of losing their language and their name of English," and longed that God might be pleased, "to discover some place unto them, though in America, . . . where they might live and comfortably subsist," and at the same time "keep their names and nation." "Jede Provinz," says Goethe, "liebt ihren Dialekt, denn er ist doch eigentlich das Element, in welchem die Seele ihren Atem schöpft." (Meyer, Volkskunde, p. 279.)

[2] In 1755 Samuel Wharton proposed, "in order to incline them to become English in education and feeling quicker," that the English language should be used in all bonds and legal instruments, and that no newspaper should be circulated among them unless accompanied by an English translation.

German only tended to strengthen the stubborn love for their language in which their Bible and hymn-books were written and in which their services were held. Indeed, the following prayer, which was introduced into the litany of the Lutheran Church, in 1786, smacks of what many would now call real fanaticism: " And since it has pleased Thee chiefly, by means of the Germans, to transform this State into a blooming garden, and the desert into a pleasant pasturage, help us not to deny our nation, but to endeavor that our youth may be so educated that German schools and churches may not only be sustained, but may attain a still more flourishing condition."

The vernacular thus religiously preserved was not the literary language of Germany, but a distinct dialect. We have seen that the vast majority of emigrants to Pennsylvania during the last century came from the various States of South Germany; the three principal ones which furnished settlers being the Palatinate, Würtemberg, and Switzerland. The inhabitants of these three form two ethnical entities which are more or less closely allied, Würtemberg and Switzerland being practically pure Alemannic, while the Palatinate is Frankish with a strong infusion of

Alemannic blood in certain parts thereof.[3]
Hence it follows that the Pennsylvania-German
dialect is a mixture of Frankish and Alemannic.
Of course there are subdivisions in these dialects,
the Swabian of Würtemberg being different from
that of Switzerland, and the mixed speech of the
Palatinate different from both.[4] The Pennsylvania German, then, has as a basis certain characteristics derived from all these dialects, modi-
fied and harmonized, many of the original differences having in course of time been so transformed that to-day the dialect is in general
homogeneous.

The accurate study of any dialect is one of
great difficulty, and should only be undertaken
by a specialist who has been thoroughly trained
in the subject of phonetics and who has made a
long and careful personal study of the facts on
the spot. This is not the place, nor is the writer
competent, to give a full treatment of this interesting dialect. There are some facts, however,
which are easily understood and which at the
same time form the most striking characteristics.

[3] See Riehl, p. 105 ff.
[4] See Paul's Grundriss der Germanischen Philologie, vol.
I. pp. 538–540 ; also Riehl, Pfälzer, p. 273 ff. The variations
in the dialect of the Palatinate may be studied in the four
"Volksdichter" Kobell, Nadler, Schandein, and Lennig.

Such are the following: *o* (more or less open) takes the place of the German *a* and *aa*, as in *schlof* (*schlaf*), *froge* (*fragen*), *woge* (*waagen*), *jor* (*jahr*), *wor* (*wahr*); *e* is used for German *ei* and *äu*, as *del* (*theil*), *hem* (*heim*), *bem* (*bäume*).[5] As in all German dialects, the mixed vowels are simplified, *ö* becoming *e* (*here*=*hören*, *he*=*höhe*, *bes*=*böse*), and *ü* becoming *i* (*bicher*=*bücher*, *brick*=*brücke*, *ivver*= *über*, etc.). The above vowel changes are extensively used; less frequent are the changes of *eu* in a few words to *ei* (*feier*=*feuer*, *scheier*= *scheuer*), and of *ei* and *ai* to *oy* (*moy*=*mai*, *oy*=*ei*, *woy*=*weihe*). A very interesting phenomenon is the influence of *r* on the preceding *i* or *e* (*arve* =*erbe*, *zwarch*=*zwerg*, *zarkel*=*zirkel*, *karch*= *kirche*.) Even the vowel *u* in some words undergoes a similar change (*dawrsch*=*durst*, *fawrch*= *furcht*, *kawrz*=*kurz*). In some cases an inorganic vowel is developed between a liquid and the following consonant (*milich*=*milch*, *marikt* =*markt*, *starick*=*stark*, *barik*=*berg*).

In regard to the consonant-system the following peculiarities may be noted: *g* between two

---

[5] In many words there is a wavering in this use of *e;* thus we find both *Kled* and *Kleid;* and especially are the suffixes *heit* and *keit* heard more often than *het* or *ket*. (Learned.) So also we find the umlaut of *Maus* = *Meis*, *Haus* = *Heiser*, etc. (Haldeman, p. 14.)

vowels and after *r* becomes *y* (*morye*=*morgen*, *reye*=*regen*); *b* between vowels becomes *v* (*geve* =*geben*, *selver*=*selber*); *b* and *p*, *t* and *d*, *g* and *k* are often interchanged (*babier*=*papier*, *del*=*theil*, *klick*=*glück*); *pf* is simplified to *p* (*pund*=*pfund*, *pluk*=*pflug*, ˙*scheppe*=*schöpfen*); *nn*=*nd* (*finne*= finden, *gfunne*=*gefunden*, *nunner*=*hinunter*); final *n* of inflections is lacking (*gucke*=*gucken*, *rechne* =*rechnen*).

Syntax is freer than in German: as in the dialect of the Palatinate, the perfect tense is regularly used for the imperfect; nominative and accusative are generally confused; the genitive is used only in compounds and adverbs, its place being taken in other constructions by *von* or by the article with the possessive pronoun.

Such are some of the most striking characteristics of the Pennsylvania-German dialect, in regard to those features which it inherits from Germany and Switzerland. But that which stamps it with especial peculiarity are the changes it has undergone under the influence of English. It was only natural that, coming to a strange land, surrounded by people speaking another language, the Germans should borrow new words, especially such as expressed things and ideas which were new to them. These words were either very familiar or technical, things they had **to** buy and sell, objects of the experiences of daily life, such as *stohr, boggy, fens, endorse,* etc. The newspapers abound in curious compounds like *eisenstove, küchenranges, parlor-oefen, carving-messer, sattler-hartwaaren, gäuls-blänkets* (horse-blankets), *frähm-sommerhaus, flauer-bärrel,*[6] etc. Many of these importations are taken without much change, as *office, operate, schquier,* etc. Many, however, are hybrid words, some with German prefix and English root (*abstarte*=start off, *abseine*=sign away, *auspicke*=pick out, *austeire* = tire out, *ferboddere* = bother); others with English root and German suffix (*hickerniss*= hickory-nuts, *krickli*=little creek); still more curious is the expression of the English idea in German (*gutgucklich*=good-looking, *hemgemacht* home-made).[7]

The interest—that is, the literary and philo-

---

[6] The last four words are taken from the Reading *Adler,* Feb. 27, 1900. This paper has been in existence 104 years, and is still read by the Berks County farmer with something of the same feeling with which the London merchant reads his *Times.*

[7] Further examples may be found in Haldeman and Learned. *I*nteresting parallels to this curious mingling of *E*nglish and German are presented in the law French of *E*ngland of the sixteenth century, where we find such expressions as "walke in le lane," "il dig up un clod del terre," "l'owner del Park vient al gate del Park pur hunter," etc. See article in North Amer. Review, vol. LI. (written by Longfellow).

logical interest—in dialects is something modern, showing itself not only in the investigations of philology, but also in the field of literature, and to-day any cleverly written piece of fiction is sure of at least temporary popularity if written in dialect. It is doubtless due to this impulse that there has arisen in the last thirty or forty years a small body of literature in the Pennsylvania-German dialect.

Dr. Philip Schaff is said to have been the first to encourage the publication of such dialect literature; it was he who, among others, urged Harbaugh to publish his poems, and the first poem printed in the Pennsylvania-German dialect appeared in the *Kirchenfreund*, 1849, at that time edited by Dr. Schaff.[8] Since that time a considerable number of persons have tried their hands at this modest kind of composition. The Nestor of such persons to-day is Mr. E. H. Rauch, who, under the *nom de plume* of Pit Schweffelbrenner, for many years has written articles, mostly humorous, for the Carbon *Democrat* and other papers; and who in 1879 published his Pennsylvania Dutch Handbook, containing a

---

[8] This was an "Abendlied," beginning "Morgets scheent die Sun so schö," by the Reverend Rondthaler, a Moravian missionary. (See Life of Schaff, by his son, p. 142.)

vocabulary with practical exercises and samples of dialect literature.

In poetry much more of a higher sort has been written, generally, however, in the form of translations from English, and of "occasional" poetry, appearing for the most part in newspapers or recited on festive occasions. In general we notice that this poetry lacks something of the spontaneity that marks true "Volkspoesie," such as we find in the works of Hebel, Nadler, and Kobel. The life of the Palatine or Swiss farmer is more individual than that of the Pennsylvania German of to-day, and the poets of the Fatherland give full expression to this life in all its varied aspects, humorous as well as pathetic. Most of the poetry written in Pennsylvania German has been written by men who have been educated in English schools and colleges,—who are largely professional men, lawyers, teachers, ministers, and journalists,—and who are thoroughly identified with American ideals. Naturally, then, such poetry cannot be simple and naïve as that written by the German "Volksdichter."

The two most voluminous writers of verse are Henry Harbaugh and H. L. Fisher. The latter, a lawyer of York, has published two volumes, "'S Alt Marik-Haus mittes in d'r Schtadt" and "Kurzweil und Zeitvertrieb," in which he gives a picture of the life of the Pennsylvania German farmer fifty years ago, describing among other things old customs, superstitions, work in field and house, planting, harvesting, threshing, beating hemp and spinning flax; the joys, toils, and pleasures of the farmer's life,—butcherings, butter-boilings, huskings, and quilting-parties. Much of the contents of the volumes, however, consists of imitations of German originals, or translations from English and especially American poetry.

The most original of these writers, and one who possessed genuine poetic gift, was the Rev. Henry Harbaugh, a prominent clergyman in the Reformed Church, who was born October 28, 1817, near Waynesboro', Franklin County, Pa., and died December 28, 1867.[9] He was an industrious writer in English, especially in the field of local church history. His Life of Michael Schlatter, and the series of Fathers of the Reformed Church projected by him, are standard works on those subjects. He also composed a number of hymns, some of which are sung by all Christian denominations.[10] For several years he had pub-

[9] His life, written by his son, has recently been published.
[10] The best known is that beginning,

"Jesus, I live to Thee,
The loveliest and best."

lished a number of dialect poems in the *Guardian;* he had often been urged to gather them in a volume, but died before this was done. In 1870 a collection of his Pennsylvania German poetry, including English translations of several of the poems, was published by Rev. B. Bausman, under the title of " Harbaugh's Harfe." The best known of these poems is " Das Alt Schulhaus an der Krick," the first stanza of which is as follows:

> " Heit is 's 'xäctly zwansig Johr,
> Dass ich bin owwe naus ;
> Nau bin ich widder lewig z'rick
> Un schteh am Schulhaus an d'r Krick,
> Juscht neekscht an's Dady's Haus."

In " Der Alte Feierheerd " the charms of a wood-fire are thus expressed:

> " Nau wammer Owets sitzt un gukt
> Wie's doch dort in de Kohle schpukt !
> Es glieht un schtrahlt—weiss, schwarz un roth—
> Nau gans lewendig, un nau dodt ;
> M'r gukt un denkt—m'r werd gans schtill,
> Un kann juscht sehne was m'r will."

The following titles will indicate the character of Harbaugh's poetry in general: " Das Krischkindel," " Die Alt Miehl," " Busch un Schtedel " (Town and Country), " Der Kerchegang in Alter Zeit," " Will Widder Buwele Sei'," etc. The poem entitled " Heemweh " expresses the feeling of sadness that comes over the man of middle life on returning after a long absence to the scenes of his youth. There is genuine poetic sentiment in such lines as the following:

> "Ich wees net, soll ich nei' in's Haus,
>   Ich zitter an d'r Dheer!
> Es is wol alles voll inseid
>   Un doch is alles leer!
> 's net meh heem, wie's eemol war,
>   Un kann's ah nimme sei';
> Was naus mit unsere Eltere geht
>   Kummt ewig nimme nei'!
> Die Freide hot der Dodt geärnt,
>   Das Trauerdheel is mei'!"

Most recent of the published volumes of Pennsylvania-German verse is a little book, attractively printed, entitled "Drauss un Deheem," by Mr. Charles C. Ziegler, a Harvard graduate of 1883. Here the homely and quaint dialect serves as a medium for college poetry in the form of rondeaus, sonnets, etc. Especially interesting is a poem, "Zum Denkmal," an imitation in sentiment and metrical form of Tennyson's "In Memoriam." [11] Those who wish to see how a

[11] The following lines will illustrate what is said above :

> "Dar Sud Wind bringt de Mensche Muth
>   Un weckt die Aerd vum Winter-Schlof,
>   Ar haucht uf Barrick un Feld un Grofe
> 'N warmer Duft, 'n siissi Gluth.

> "Die ganz Nadur fihlt sei Gewalt,
>   Juscht net die Dodte : schtumm un daab
>   Un reglos bleiwe sie im Graab,
> Sie bleiwe u'bewegt un kalt.

quaint dialect can adapt itself to modern poetic themes should read this little book.

This dialect literature, however, is of very recent origin; and as the present book aims chiefly at describing the Pennsylvania Germans as they were in the eighteenth century, the literary activity of our ancestors has more real connection with our theme. This activity, indeed, is more extensive than some would suppose. Of course it goes without saying that whatever was published then was not in dialect, but in literary German.

At that time the intellectual interests of the Germans of Pennsylvania, as well as those in the Fatherland, were almost entirely of a theological nature; hence it happens that some of the earliest products of the Pennsylvania-German press were devotional and religious books or pamphlets, largely of a polemical character. Thus the first German book published in Pennsylvania was Conrad Beissel's " Büchlein vom Sabbath," [12]

> " Los'vun de Eis-Kett laaft die Grick,
> Es blihe weiss die Eppelbleem,
> Die Veggel kumme widder heem —
> Alles geliebtes kummt zerick.
>
> " Juscht net die Dodte—un ich guck
> Iwwer dar Himmel 'naus,—die Dräne
> Beweise wen ich winsch ze sehne
> Weit liewer a's daer Frihlingsschmuck."

[12] Published by Andrew Bradford in 1728. See Seidensticker, "The First Century of German Printing in America."

which, in the words of the Chronicon Ephratense, "led to the public adoption of the seventh
day for divine service." The next year George
Michael Weiss published through Bradford a
polemic against the New-Born, a sect of sancti-
ficationists which, under the leadership of Matthias Bauman, deeply stirred the Germans of
Montgomery County. These books began the
long series of theological literature in Pennsylvania which, receiving a new and strong impulse
through the coming of Zinzendorf, has in one
form or another, by Dunkard, Mennonite, Lutheran, or Reformed, come down to our own day.

Original composition in verse at that time was
chiefly in the form of hymns,[13] of which a considerable number were written. Most of the
brethren of the Ephrata Community turned their
hand to this kind of poetry, the most voluminous
being Beissel himself. As early as 1730, Benjamin Franklin published a book entitled " Gött-
liche Liebes- und Lobesgethöne," containing 62
hymns, 31 by Beissel and the rest by his asso-
ciates; while in 1739 Christopher Sauer published a large hymn-book entitled " Zionitischer

---

[13] This is likewise true of Germany at this time. What
Scherer says of the hymns in that country applies equally well
to early German-American hymnology. (See Scherer, Geschichte der deutschen Litteratur, p. 340 ff.)

Weyrauchshügel," containing 654 hymns in 33 divisions, " Each inscribed with a heading as fantastical as the general title." [14]

The poetical talent of Beissel, as shown in these hymns, was of a low order, and probably not nearly so great as his musical talent; they are filled with fantastic ideas, and couched in mystical and often obscure language in which sensuous love is used to express spiritual experience. They are quite in harmony, however, with the literary taste of the day in Germany and Switzerland.[15]

The most important of all the earliest literary men was Francis Daniel Pastorius, the founder of Germantown. We have already seen that he was a man of learning, writing fluently in a number of languages. He was an industrious writer on a number of subjects both in prose and poetry. Only a few, however, of his writings have ap-

[14] This includes all the hymns written by Beissel and others and published by Franklin in 1730, 1732, 1736, together with a large amount of material obtained elsewhere, especially from the " Kleine Davidische Psalterspiel," the hymn-book of the *I*nspirationists in Germany and published by Sauer in 1744.

[15] Among other writers of hymns in Pennsylvania were Peter Böhler, Zinzendorf, Spangenberg, Nitschman (all Moravians), Helmuth, Muhlenberg, Kunze, Weiser (Lutherans). See, for a discussion of this subject, Haussmann, German-American Hymnology, 1683–1800.

peared in print, and the couple of German books which he wrote were published abroad. He left a number of manuscripts, most of which are lost, but a list of whose titles is found in the " Bee-hive," a strange conglomeration compiled for his children, being a sort of cyclopædia of history, biography, ethics, religion, and language. It also contains a collection of inscriptions, epitaphs, proverbs, poetry (original and selected), pithy sayings, acrostics, etc.[16]

This native literary product, however, did not suffice to supply the demand for literature on the part of the early German settlers. Whatever else may be said about their education, they must have been great readers. This is seen in the number of books imported as well as printed in the commonwealth itself. The hymn-books prepared by Beissel and others were used by the Dunkards, while the Mennonites had the venerable Ausbund, which was printed a number of

---

[16] The full title is "Alvearum Apiculæ Germanopolitanum Anglicanum." The poetry of Pastorius was mostly doggerel, as the following sample will show:

> "This book seems tall and small,
> Of no esteem at all;
> Yet I would very fain
> That any who doth find
> The same would be so kind
> To send it me again."

times by Sauer and is still in use by the Amish;[17] the Schwenckfelders likewise had their own book, containing a number of original hymns. For a long time the Lutherans and Reformed imported the Marburger hymn-book, which was later reprinted many times by Sauer. These books were not merely used in church, but were read and pored over and committed to memory almost as much as the Bible.

We shall see later how eager the Germans were to obtain copies of the Bible; in the correspondence with Holland this subject constantly occurs, and it was only natural that as soon as Sauer had established his printing-press on a firm basis he should think of printing a German Bible,—not for gain, he says himself, but "to the honor of the German people." The glory of the German press in America is the quarto Bible of Sauer, the first one printed in the New World in any European language, and of which three editions were published before the

[17] Ausbund, das ist : *E*tliche schöne christliche Lieder wie sie in dem Gefängnüss zu Bassau in dem Schloss von den Schweitzer-Brüdern und von andern rechtglaubigen Christen hin und her gedichtet worden." Wackernagel dates this book from 1583 ; *E*gli in his Züricher Wiedertäufer is inclined to give it an earlier origin. In the edition of Sauer valuable biographical details are given of the ancestors of many Lancaster County families.

first English Bible appeared in Philadelphia in 1782.[18]

Of the many books of devotional literature published in Pennsylvania,[19] the most interesting is the translation of Van Bragt's " Blutige Schauplatz oder Martyrer Spiegel " into German by members of the Ephrata Community and published by them in 1748.[20] It was really a re-

[18] Sauer's third edition came out in 1776. For a detailed account of Sauer's Bible see John Wright, *Early Bibles of America*, p. 31. The activity of the German press is a striking proof of the intelligence of the people and their interest in theological literature. Franklin says that in 1753 there were two German presses in Pennsylvania, two half-German, while only two were entirely English. (*Works*, II. p. 297.)

[19] Each denomination had its own especial books of devotion,—the Mennonites having Menno Simon's *Fundament* and Dirck Philip's *Enchiridion* in addition to the Martyr-book described above; the Reformed had Stark's *Gebet-Buch*, while the Lutherans had Arndt's *Wahres Christenthum* and *Paradies-Gärtlein*. The latter was believed to be proof against fire, and Sachse gives an instance in proof thereof, which occurred near Womelsdorf, Berks Co. A similar superstition is alluded to in a letter by Swedenborg's father, whose house burned down in 1712: "The fire broke out in my study, which was all ablaze when we got to it, with my library and MSS., but, strange to say, the Garden of Paradise by J. Arndt, and my own catechism, were found in the ashes with only their covers singed." (White's *Life of Swedenborg*, vol. I. p. 33.)

[20] This book gives the persecutions and sufferings of those Christians who were opposed to war, from the time of the apostles down to the Swiss Mennonitesin the seventeenth century.

markable achievement for a small religious community in the heart of a new colony to translate, print, and bind the largest book published in America. It took fifteen men three years to complete the task, the first part being published in 1748, the second in 1749. The price was 20 shillings.[21]

The inhabitants of the city in modern times can have no conception of the importance of the almanac for the farmer of a hundred years ago. In Germany it occupied a place beside the Bible and the hymn-book, and was constantly consulted before any of the important affairs of life were undertaken. These old German almanacs were the repositories of all the superstitions which still flourished in the country and which, banished from regular literature, found a refuge here.[22] Here were given the proper times for sowing, reaping, building fences, shingling the roof, and even hair-cutting and bleeding, together with the *materia medica* of the Bauer,— the medicinal plants which, in the absence of

[21] The cause of the translation at this time was the approach of the French and Indian War ; the Mennonites believed that their principles against the bearing of arms would subject them once more to persecution, and desired to fortify themselves by reading of the heroic deeds of their ancestors. For description of this remarkable book see Penn. Mag., vol. v.

[22] See Riehl, Kulturstudien, p. 43 ff.

regular physicians, played so large a part in the treatment of ailments. These almanacs were very popular in Pennsylvania, especially those of Christopher Sauer, which, beginning in August, 1738 (the first book he published), lasted for forty years, and then were continued by other firms. For many years Sauer's almanacs were the only ones printed in German, and were used in South Carolina, Georgia, and other Southern States where German farmers then lived. Franklin published a German almanac for a short time, but it soon died a natural death; Armbrüster, Miller, and others were more fortunate, but Sauer's was the most popular as long as it lasted.

Newspapers were not so plentiful one hundred years ago as they are to-day; in 1775 there were only 37 in the American Colonies. Of these 14 were in New England, 4 in New York, and 9 in Pennsylvania. If we take the number of newspapers as an indication of the intelligence of the people, the Pennsylvania Germans do not suffer much in comparison with their English neighbors. According to McCrady[23] the average number of inhabitants to support a newspaper in the above year was 64,000; now of the nine in Pennsylvania in 1775 two were German, which

[23] History of South Carolina ; see Literature, Sept. 8, 1899.

should give the German population at 128,000, which is not far from the real figures. Indeed the assumption that the Germans were great readers can alone account for the instant success of Sauer's newspaper, "Der Hoch-Deutsch Pennsylvanische Geschieht-Schreiber oder Sammlung wichtiger Nachrichten aus dem Natur- und Kirchenreich," the first number of which appeared August 20, 1739. This paper became very popular, having in its flourishing period four thousand subscribers.[24] Towards the end of the century the number of German newspapers rapidly increased, being published not only in Philadelphia, but in Lancaster, Reading, Allentown, and other cities. Many of them, still in German, exist to-day.[25]

[24] Wright says ten thousand.

[25] In this connection, a word or two, perhaps, ought to be said of that kind of literature which, like the common law of England, exists unwritten. Proverbs were very popular among the Pennsylvania Germans, and in certain districts are so still, Many of them are the same as we find in English, such as. "Out of the frying-pan into the fire," "The burnt child dreads the fire," etc. Some are, however, peculiar to themselves. Such are the following : "En blindti Sau, findt â alsamôl 'n Echel"; "En fauler Esel shaft sich gschwinter dodt as 'n shmärder"; "Der Appel folt net weit fom Bom"; "Sauerkraut und Speck dreebt alle Sorge weck."

> "Wer sich nehra will mit Fisha und Yawga,
> Muss ferissene Husse drawga."

For further examples see Mathews and Hungerford's Hist,

It is a difficult thing for people of any age or country to give a just estimate of another nation, with whose language and customs they are unacquainted. What always happens took place in Pennsylvania one hundred and fifty years ago. The Germans were misunderstood in many ways by their English-speaking neighbors. Owing to the fear on the part of the latter of being swamped by foreigners, to the suspicions aroused by Jesuit machinations, and to political prejudice and passion, they were accused, among other things, of stupidity, obstinacy, and ignorance. In regard to the latter accusation some light is afforded by a letter written to Peter Collinson by Benjamin Franklin in 1753. From this letter it appears that in the mind of Franklin, at least, "ignorance" and "ignorance of the English language" are identical terms; for he goes on to say: "Few of their children in the country know English. They import many books from Germany, and of the six printing-houses in the province two are entirely German, two half German, half English, and but two are entirely English. They have one German newspaper and one half German." Surely a people which had as many printing-presses and newspapers as the English, who outnumbered them two to one, were not ignorant in the proper sense of that term.[26]

Careful study of the facts will show the true state of affairs to have been something as follows. The mass of the early German settlers of Pennsylvania, while not highly educated, were not ignorant or illiterate. The proportion of those who could read and write was probably as large as that in rural New England and New York, at least in the pioneer days of those colonies.[27] All had received at least the elements of education in the Fatherland, in accordance with the universal custom in Protestant Germany of uniting

[26] Franklin, Works (ed. Ford), vol. II. The political bias is seen in the following words from the same letter : " For I remember when they modestly declined intermeddling with our elections ; but now they come in droves and carry all before them, except in one or two counties."

[27] " The people of Colonial New England were not all well-educated, nor were all their country schools better than old field schools. The farmer's boy, who was taught for two winter months by a man and two summer months by a woman, seldom learned more in the district school than how to read, write, and cipher." (Fiske, Old Virginia and her Neighbors, vol. II. p. 251.)

" There was often a disposition on the part of the town meetings to shirk the appropriation of a sum of money for school purposes. . . . In those dark days of New England, there might now and then be found in rural communities men of substance who signed deeds and contracts with their mark." (Ibid.)

education and religion.[28]   In the early days of
pioneer life in the wilderness of interior Pennsylvania, they lacked both schools and books, a
condition of affairs, however, more and more
remedied after the third decade of the eighteenth
century.   The early Philadelphia press was busy
printing Bibles, hymn-books, the standard books
of devotion, and even school-books.[29]   The
reading of these books, the committing to memory of extended passages of Scripture and of the
hymn-book, the rapid spread of the newspaper,
which we shall notice elsewhere, must presup-
pose a certain degree of education—an education
which, while not broad nor deep, was practical
both in religious and secular affairs.

There was, however, a comparatively large
number of the German pioneers who seemed
to possess what might be called learning.
Even among unprofessional people we find

[28] " Seit der Reformation waren wenigstens in allen Kirch-
dörfern Schulen, die Lehrer oft Theologen." (Freytag, vol.
III. p. 106.)

[29] The first book on pedagogy published in America was
by Christopher Dock, written in 1750, but printed by Sauer
in 1770 after the death of the writer.   Dock was an interesting character ; he advocated correspondence between the
pupils of different schools as a means of education, thus an-
ticipating the modern system of correspondence between the
school-youth of France, Germany, England, and America.
(See Pennypacker, Historical and Biographical Sketches.)

traces of classical learning ; thus Johannes Kolb, a weaver of Germantown, had a copy of Erasmus in Latin,[30] which he had bought from his brother; and a Schwenckfelder, named Schultz, had a well-thumbed copy of a Latin grammar.[31] The earliest settlers were under the direction of some of the most learned men of the time. We have seen that the Frankfort Company consisted of a number of well-educated and highborn people; their agent, Pastorius, we have already spoken of. Of the company of mystics who came over in 1694 most were university men. Zimmermann, who had planned the colony, was called by Arnold "Ein grundgelehrter Astrologus," etc. Johann Kelpius, his successor as leader of the colony, was the son of a clergyman, and a Doctor of Philosophy of Tübingen; Henry Bernard Köster had studied at the gymnasium of Bremen and at Frankfort; Daniel Falckner was the son and grandson of clergymen and was himself educated for the ministry; his brother had been a student in Halle and had left home in order to "escape the burden of the pastorate." Finally, Peter Miller, at one time prior

[30] Pennypacker, Germantown, picture opp. p. 194.
[31] Now in charge of Dr. C. D. Hartranft, president of Hartford Theological Seminary, who has been engaged for many years on a complete edition of the works of Schwenckfeld.

of Ephrata, was a very learned man and often came to Philadelphia to attend the meetings of the Philosophical Society; he is said to have translated the Declaration of Independence into seven different languages.[32] Of course the regularly ordained ministers of the Lutheran and Reformed churches [33] were men of education, as that was a necessary qualification in Germany for those who entered the ministry.

The subject of education among the Germans was the cause of a great deal of acrimonious discussion towards the middle of the last century, and, as usual in such cases, many false and inaccurate statements were made. Politics both of State and Church had much to do with this agitation. There seems to have been a genuine fear, however, on the part of the English inhabitants that the French were endeavoring to enlist the sympathies of the Germans in their efforts at supremacy over the whole of western America.

[32] Miller applied to the Scotch Synod for ordination. "We gave him," says Andrews, "a question to discuss about justification, and he answered it in a whole sheet in a very notable manner. He speaks Latin as readily as we do our vernacular tongue."

[33] The Synods of Holland sent Schlatter to Germany and Switzerland to seek ministers for Pennsylvania who should be "orthodox, learned, pious." (Harbaugh, Life of Schlatter, p. 232.)

Indeed, we have documentary evidence that such attempts were made. In the examination of William Johnson in 1756 testimony was given to the effect that a certain priest, Neal, insinuated that it would be better to live under French government, as religion would be free, and told them to get arms and be ready to join the French and Indians.[34] So, too, we read in an intercepted letter written from Canada in 1756 that the Moravians were true Roman Catholics [*sic*] and that the writer was persuaded that " they would rather serve his royal Majesty." [35]

That there was no need for anxiety goes without saying; the Germans were, as they afterwards proved, too loyal to listen to any appeals on the part of the French. They could not have forgotten that France was chiefly responsible for the desolation of their own homes in Germany. Besides, the Lutherans and Reformed, who had come to America to escape the persecution of a Catholic government, were not likely to put themselves in the same predicament by espousing the cause of a country whose revocation of the Edict of Nantes had driven all Prot-

[34] Penn. Arch., 1st Ser., vol. III. p. 16.

[35] Amer. Hist. Assoc. Reports, vol. I. p. 663. The mysterious journeys of the Moravians to the wilderness, the strange practices of the *E*phrata Community, all helped to spread this suspicion.

estants from France and even from Canada. Such insinuations roused the indignation of all classes of Germans. The German Protestants of Philadelphia County made a vigorous protest against all attacks on their loyalty.[36]

These suspicions are now seen by us to have been utterly unfounded, and yet it was perhaps not unnatural that the English should entertain such fears in regard to foreigners, of whose customs and religion they were so little instructed. French rule in America meant not only political supremacy, but the extension of Catholicism wherever that rule extended. It had not been many years before that England had driven out the popish dynasty of the Stuarts; the " Scarlet Woman " had not lost her terrors, and the cry of " no popery " had not yet died out in the land.[37]

Owing to such fears utterly exaggerated statements were made regarding the number of Catholics among the Germans; the Moravians were accused of collusion with the French, and the monastery at Ephrata was declared to be

[36] Penn. Arch., 1st Ser., vol. II. p. 201 : "How, therefore, can any man of due Reason think, much less say, that this same people were anyways inclined to submit themselves again under a Romish slavery upheld by a French king ? "

[37] " The clamors against popery are as loud as ever." (Letter by Dan. Dulaney, Dec. 9, 1755, in Penn. Mag., vol. III. p. 11.)

ruled, if not directly by the pope, yet according to popish rules.[38] William Smith in his " Brief State of the Province of Pennsylvania " declared that one-fourth of the Germans were Catholics, while the rest were liable to be seduced by every enterprising Jesuit. As a matter of actual fact, out of the total population in 1757 only 1365 were Catholics, of whom 923 were Germans.[39]

These were the facts, or rather the fears, that underlay the formation of the " Society for the Promotion of the Knowledge of God among the Germans." A pamphlet written by Dr. Smith set forth the object of the society, and a large sum of money was subscribed for the purpose of founding English schools in the various German settlements. The statements as to the ignorance of the Germans made in the above pamphlet were so false as to draw out indignant protests both from the Reformed and the Lutherans.[40] From the very beginning both these denominations had schools

[38] These suspicions finally induced the government to send a committee to Ephrata, but Beissel and Miller easily showed how unfounded they were.

[39] Penn. Arch., 1st Ser., vol. III. p. 144.

[40] There is no reason to suppose that these statements were deliberate falsehoods ; as usually happens in such cases, the English had but little accurate knowledge concerning their

connected with the various churches, and no community held religious services without at the same time taking thought for the religious and secular instructions of their children.[41] In some places there were schoolmasters even before regular pastors, and one of their duties was to read the services on Sunday.[42]

While of course in the early decades of the century schools were few and scattered, and while even in Muhlenberg's time he could still complain of the want of good schools, yet the consideration of a few facts will show that in general the Germans were at least no worse off than their Quaker fellows, or than was natural in a new and wild country. As early as 1748 Jacob Loeser was teacher of the Lutheran church in Lancaster, in summer teaching fifty or sixty pupils, in winter eighty or ninety. In fact we are told that the school grew so large that sixteen English children had to be dismissed.[43] As

German neighbors. Moreover, the desire to make a successful appeal for funds almost necessarily led to exaggeration.

[41] Thus, in 1730, the settlers in Tulpehocken built log schoolhouses near the present Reed Church, with Caspar Leutbecker as schoolmaster.

[42] See the agreement between Hoffman and the Reformed Church in Lancaster in 1747, in which he agrees to "serve as chorister, read sermons on Sunday, and to keep school every day in the year as is the usual custom."

[43] Handschuh, in Hall. Nach.

to the curriculum of these schools, we get a glimpse thereof in the records of the time. The teacher of the Reformed church in Philadelphia was to teach the children reading, writing, singing, and to lead a godly life; he was to instruct them in the articles of the Reformed faith, in the Ten Commandments, and to make them commit to memory passages of Scripture.[44]

That the Germans were not unprovided with schools for proper instruction in their own language the following unprejudiced witness may serve as proof: " The country for miles around this town is thick peopled, but few else than Germans and Quakers, the former being computed at twelve to one of all other nations together, and seem to be abundantly well provided in teachers of one denomination or another. . . . They might be at no loss for English schoolmasters, yet they choose to send their children rather to German schools, which they have everywhere in great plenty." [45]

Although Muhlenberg and Schlatter were members of the committee, and although schools were established in Lancaster, Reading,

[44] Wickersham, Hist. of Education in Penn.
[45] Letter of Rev. Alexander Murray, Secretary of the Society for Propagation of the Gospel in Foreign Parts, dated at Reading, April 9, 1763.

York, etc., the movement soon failed ignomin-
iously. Christopher Sauer threw the whole
weight of his personality against it, and his paper
vigorously assailed the motives which he declared underlay the movement. According to
him the motives were two: first, to draw the
German vote away from the Quakers;[46] second, to attract the Lutherans to the Church of
England.[47] After a few years the schools were

[46] See Gordon, Hist. of Pennsylvania, pp. 328, 9. Sauer
seems to have been right to a certain extent. *Only* political prejudice could make Smith utter such evident falsehoods as the following: "One-half the people are an uncultivated race of Germans liable to be seduced by every enterprising Jesuit, having almost no Protestant clergy among
them to put them on their guard and warn them against
popery." (A Brief State of the Province of Penn. (Sabin Re-
print), p. 19.) And again: "The Germans, instead of being
a peaceful and industrious people as before, now finding themselves of such consequence, are grown self-willed·and tur-
bulent, . . . will soon be able to give us law and language or
else, by joining with the French, to eject all *E*nglish inhabitants." (p. 31.)

[47] This actually happened with many churches in New York,
Maryland, and Virginia, as well as with the Swedish Lutherans
in Pennsylvania. At that time both churches were closely
connected. George I. was still in private a Lutheran, not being willing to renounce his religion for a crown. In Pennsylvania and New York they worked in harmony, and in 1797
a resolution was passed under Dr. Kunze "that, on account of
an intimate relation subsisting between the *E*nglish Episcopalian and Lutheran churches, . . . this consistory will never
acknowledge a newly erected Lutheran church in places where

given up. Schlatter lost his influence among his countrymen largely through his connection with the matter.

The gist of the much-mooted school question at that time was a question of language. The English not unnaturally looked upon this as an obstacle to the speedy and complete assimilation of the Germans to the English community, which in those days of suspicion of all things foreign was looked upon as a consummation devoutly to be wished. The Germans have been much blamed in this affair, and doubtless it would have been better **for** them if by means of these schools they had become Anglicized a generation or two earlier. Yet their feeling was a natural one: they did not want to give up their language; they had schools of their own which satisfied them. They saw no reason for the change, and hence were easily led to see wrong motives in what purported to be, and in the case of many people really was, philanthropy. They were, more-

the members may partake of the services of the said *E*nglish *E*piscopal church." (Jacobs, Hist. of Lutherans, p. 318.) Muhlenberg was strongly attached to the *E*piscopalians and at one time disposed to unite with them. Cf. also letter of Thos. Barton in 1764: "The Germans in general are well affected to the Church of *E*ngland, and might easily be brought over to it. A law obliging them to give their children an *E*nglish education . . . would soon have this effect."

over, indignant at being treated as ignorant
boors, and were proud and independent enough
to repudiate the idea that they should become
the recipients of charity.[48]

Nearly seventy-five years later a similar contest arose in Pennsylvania over the introduction
of the common-school system; and here again
the Germans largely opposed the movement and
received their full share of obloquy as being opposed to education. But the impartial student of the facts will find, not justification,
yet at least some excuse for their taking such a
stand. Their opposition to the common-school
law was due to the fact that it tended to with-
draw education from the control of the parents
and clergy. As the Hon. H. A. Muhlenberg

[48] See Harbaugh, Life of Schlatter, p. 294. "One says:
'I am conscientious in regard to having my children taught at
the expense of public charity, because I do not stand in need
of such aid, for I can pay myself.'" Muhlenberg, Schlatter,
and later Kunze were in favor of introducing the *E*nglish
language into school and church. At the very beginning of
German immigration Pastorius wrote to his children, John,
Samuel, and Henry: "Though you are (Germano sanguine
nati) of high Dutch [*sic*] parents, yet remember that your
father was naturalized and ye born in an *E*nglish colony.
Consequently each of you Anglicus natus, an *E*nglish-
man by birth. Therefore it would be a shame for you if
you should be ignorant of the *E*nglish tongue, the tongue
of your countrymen." (Pennypacker, Penn. Mag., vol. IV.
pp. I ff.)

wrote in a letter to the workingmen of Philadelphia, January 26, 1836: " The Germans of our State are not opposed to education as such, but only to any system that to them seems to trench on their parental and natural rights." They still retained the German theory of education, that the child belongs first to God, then to the parents, then to the State, the chief responsibility for their education resting on Church and parents. Their educational system was pre-eminently a religious one, which looked not only at the intellect but the soul, and had in mind not only the preparation for the life that now is, but for the life to come. An additional reason, of course, was their attachment to their own dialect, a subject which at this time was playing so important a rôle in church affairs.[49]

From the vantage-ground of the present day we believe them to have been wrong in opposing the common-school system, and they recognize it now, but it was not ignorance nor any unworthy motive which led to their opposition. Nor must it be forgotten that it was a German governor, George Wolf, who finally succeeded in effecting the adoption of the new system. In regard to the whole question of their attitude towards education, the testimony of an expert

[49] See p. 117.

in education in Pennsylvania, and one not of German descent, may fitly close this part of our discussion. Wickersham in his History of Education in Pennsylvania says: "The above facts will be sufficient to make known the deep interest in education felt by a people whose history in this respect has either been badly learned or greatly misunderstood." [50]

Hitherto we have been speaking of elementary education, in regard to which we have seen that the Germans were from the beginning anxious to provide for their children. When we come to higher education the case is different. During the eighteenth century there was little interest in colleges or universities among them. Many of the sects, especially the Dunkards and Mennonites, were opposed to it on the same grounds as the Quakers; while the vast majority of the Lutherans and Reformed were farmers and saw no reason why their children should need to know more than they did. To read and write, to know something of arithmetic, to be able to read the Bible, hymn-book, and newspaper, seemed to them all that was necessary. It was owing to this lukewarmness that Franklin College, founded at Lancaster to show, as the charter declares, the public appreciation of the services of the Ger-

[50] p. 142.

mans in the development of the State, fell to the ground in spite of the efforts of such men as Franklin, Rush, Muhlenberg, Hiester, Helmuth, and others.

In recent years, however, this state of affairs has much changed. With the growth of towns and cities, with the progress of manufactures, with the intermarriage and mingling with their neighbors, the old conservative spirit has largely passed away. Though even now some look with disfavor on higher education,[51] yet in general Pennsylvania is well provided with colleges. Such are the denominational colleges of Lebanon Valley, Ursinus, Franklin and Marshall, and many others. A large proportion of the faculty and students of the University of Pennsylvania, State College, Jefferson Medical School, etc., are of Pennsylvania-German descent. Nor are such students and teachers confined to their own State; they may be found in nearly every

---

[51] "Among the queries sent up in later years [i.e., to the Annual Meeting of the Dunkards] was one asking whether it was lawful for Brethren to establish or patronize high-schools. The reply was that Brethren should not mind *high* things, but condescend to men of low estate. The Brethren, however, continued to maintain a high-school, and have even established colleges." (Carroll, Religious Forces of the United States, p. 130.)

college of the South and West, and even of New England.

As for secondary education, perhaps no State is more energetic than Pennsylvania; nowhere are the high-schools and normal schools more numerous or better attended. The Moravian schools at Lititz and Bethlehem have for over a century been regarded as among the best in the land, and are still flourishing.[52]

[52] The interest of the Moravians in *Education* dates from early times. When Mr. Henry Dunster, president of Harvard College, who became "entangled in the snares of Anabaptism and filled the *Overseers* with uneasie fears," was forced to resign in 1654, "that brave old man Johannes Amos Comenius . . . was invited to "come over to New *England* [and illuminate this Colledge in the quality of President." (Cotton Mather, Magnalia Christi Americana, Book 4, Part I.)

CHAPTER VI.

THE RELIGIOUS LIFE.

In Chapter IV we have seen the Pennsylvania German engaged in the practical affairs of life; in Chapter V we have endeavored to describe his intellectual condition. In the present chapter we shall attempt to round out the picture by discussing his moral and religious nature.

No one who has made a careful study of the habits and customs of the German and Swiss settlers of Pennsylvania in the eighteenth century can resist the conviction that they were essentially a deeply religious people.[1] It is true that for the first two or three decades there was little or no regular religious organization, outside the various sects; it is true that many who lived far in the wilderness had lost the habit of church-going, and that many children were unbaptized and without proper religious instruction. But this was through no fault of their own, and as

[1] Even in olden times "die Deutschen waren ein sehr frommes und Gottbedürftiges Volk." (See Freytag, vol I. p. 212.)

soon as the country became sufficiently settled spontaneous efforts were made on all sides to obtain the services of pastor and schoolmaster.[2]

The testimony of men like Falckner, Weiss, and others in this matter must be taken with some degree of reserve, and their description of the religious state of their countrymen refers very largely to the anarchy which reigned in church relations rather than to general demoralization in actual living.[3] At this time the Lutheran and Reformed churches were without any organization or regular pastors, and the only religious activity was to be found among the Mennonites and the Dunkards, both of which sects made many converts among the two regular confessions. Even the testimony of Brunnholtz and Muhlenberg, later on, must be taken with caution. In their pietistic ideas and their

[2] See Harbaugh, Life of Schlatter, and Hall. Nachrichten. Schlatter tells how people would "with tears in their eyes" entreat him to assist them, etc. (p. 142.)

[3] As a sample of the sentiments of the regular clergy, take the following extract from a letter by Boehm to the Classis of Amsterdam, Nov. 12, 1730 : "By these dangerous sects an appalling number of people have been led astray. . . . The two main heretics [C. Beissel and Michael Wohlfahrt] live at Canastoka and Falkner-Schwam. Meanwhile it must be feared that if they are not opposed many poor people will be led astray by them." (Hinke, *Early* Hist. of Ref. Church in the Conestoga Valley, in the Reformed Church Record.)

eagerness to see the fruits of their labors, they unconsciously darkened the picture, while the success of the Moravians roused their ire.

We have ample evidence that, scattered as they were in the wilderness which then formed the interior counties of Pennsylvania, the people hungered and thirsted for the word of God. This is the natural explanation of the numerous revivals attending the labors of Wohlfahrt, Bauman, and Mack, and likewise explains the extraordinary success of the Ephrata Community and the Moravians, and the rise of the Dunkards,—most of the converts to whom were taken directly from the Lutherans and Reformed. When Muhlenberg came to Pennsylvania great crowds flocked to hear him,[4] and this same love for religion continued down to the end of the century, when the efforts of Boehm, Otterbein, Albright, and Winebrenner resulted in the formation of several new evangelical denominations. In fact no people in America were so subject to religious excitements as the Germans of Pennsylvania during the eighteenth century.

We read in the Hallesche Nachrichten how

[4] See Hall. Nach., *passim;* also Schlatter's Life. Handschuh writes on one occasion : "Das Volk war mit seiner besondern Aufmerksamkeit, Andacht im Singen, Ehrerbietung bei der öffentlichen Beichte auf den Knien etc., ungemein erbaulich." (H. N., I. p. 165.)

people came fifteen or twenty, nay even two hundred miles to hear sermons and receive sacrament. When Whitefield passed like a flaming comet through the colonies in 1740 he preached to thousands of Germans, who, though they could not understand English, flocked to hear the great evangelist.[5]

This deep religious nature is also shown in their reverence and love for the Bible. Those who had been able had brought with them Bibles from the Fatherland, and cherished them as the choicest of their possessions;[6] others, who were poorer or who had lost all their property in the

[5] In a letter dated April 10, 1740, Whitefield writes: "Some of the Germans in America are holy souls. They keep up a close walk with God and are remarkable for their sweetness and simplicity of behaviour. They talk little; they think much." In the Journal of his travelling-companion, William Seward, under date of April 24th we read: "Came to Christopher Wigner's plantation in Skippack, where many Dutch people are settled. . . . It was surprising to see such a multitude of people gathered together in such a wilderness country, etc. After he had done, our dear friend Peter Boehler preached in Dutch to those who could not understand English. . . . Came to Henry Anti's plantation, in Frederick Township, ten miles farther, where was also a multitude, etc. There were Germans where we dined and supped, and they pray'd and sung in Dutch as we did in English. . . . O Heavenly Musick! How sweet and delightful it is to a New-Born Soul!" (Dotterer, Hist. Notes, p. 84.) Of Antes Whitefield says he "seemed to have drunk deeply into the consolations of the Holy Spirit."

[6] Among the rare bibliographical treasures in Pennsylvania

confusion and dishonesty which so often accompanied an ocean voyage then, made every effort to get possession of the precious book. Muhlenberg tells us how even redemptioners saved their chance earnings to buy copies. One of the first things a man did on getting married was to buy a family Bible. It was to supply this universal demand that Sauer undertook to publish his famous Quarto. Nor were these Bibles mere ornaments of the centre-table; they formed the daily food of those who possessed them. The people of those days were " Bibelfest," their memories were stored with the best passages; and this is true not only of adults, but of little children as well.

The same statements apply to the hymn-book, which was held in almost the same reverence as the Bible. It was not left in the pew at church, but shared with the Holy Book the honor of being read constantly and learned by heart.[7] They

to-day are the copies of the Bible published by Froschauer of Zürich, and brought over by the early Swiss Mennonites.

[7] Many examples are given by Muhlenberg in Hall. Nach. Take as a single instance the pathetic story of the death of a six-year-old boy. When too weak himself to sing the hymns, "deren er eine schöne Anzahl gelernet," he would ask his parents to sing. " Als sein Verlangen erfüllt war, gab er seinem Vater einen liebreichen Kuss zum Abschiede, begehrte hernach wieder auf sein Bette, und indem beiderseits Eltern den Vers sungen: 'Breit aus die Flügel beide, O Jesu meine

were not only "Bibel-fest," but "Gesangbuch-fest," and in times of danger, sickness, and death comfort and strength were drawn from the grand old hymns of the Church. Many touching and inspiring stories might be told in this connection, like that of Barbara Hartman, who after many years' captivity among the Indians was restored to her mother, whom she only recognized when the latter sang to her the hymn,

"Allein und doch nicht ganz allein,
Bin ich in meiner Einsamkeit."[8]

with which she had often cradled her infant daughter to sleep; or that still more inspiring story of John Christian Schell and his wife and four sons, who kept at bay a band of sixty-four Indians and Tories all night long, shooting at them from the windows, and keeping up their courage by singing lustily Luther's old battle-hymn, "Ein feste Burg ist Unser Gott," emphasizing, we well may believe, especially the lines:

"Und wenn die Welt voll Teufel wär'
Und wollt' uns gar verschlingen,
So fürchten wir uns nicht so sehr,
Es muss uns doch gelingen."[9]

Freude, Und nimm dein Küchlein ein,' entschlief er sanft und stille in seinem Erlöser." (vol. II. p. 468.)

[8] This interesting story is given in detail in Hall. Nach., vol. II. p. 479 ff.

[9] Kapp, p. 262 ff. It is a satisfaction to know that this brave family was rescued on the following day.

What has been stated above is perhaps only another way of saying that the whole religious life of the early Pennsylvania Germans was strongly marked by pietism. This movement, which we have spoken of before, was not a propagation of dogma or a new ecclesiastical polity, but the immediate application of the teaching of Christ to the heart and conduct, a revolt against the formalism of the orthodox church; it was to Germany what Methodism became later to England.

It is interesting to note the development of pietism in Pennsylvania. Almost all those who came over in the early part of the century were affected by it; nay, the Frankfort Company was formed by the members of one of the so-called *Collegia Pietatis* founded by Spener; hence Germantown owes its foundation to this movement. Zinzendorf and the Moravians, the Schwarzenau Baptists, the Schwenckfelders, Otterbein and Boehm, who founded the United Brethren, and Muhlenberg, who had been educated at Halle, then the centre of the movement in Germany,—all were thoroughly imbued with the spirit of pietism. The same tendency, carried to excess and manifesting itself in mysticism, is seen in the Society of the Woman in the Wilderness founded by Kelpius, and in the Ephrata Community.

The stream of emotional religion, thus having its source in Germany, gained new strength in Pennsylvania, where all conditions were favorable to its development. While in Germany it practically died out as a force before the end of the century, in the New World it flowed on in new channels, and finally culminated in the founding of several new denominations, which to-day are strong in numbers and influence.[10]

The great majority of Germans in colonial Pennsylvania belonged to the two principal confessions, Lutheran and Reformed, the latter coming chiefly from Switzerland and the Palatinate, the former from Würtemberg and other parts of Germany. Their numbers in the Quaker colony were nearly equal.

One phenomenon which a century ago attracted widespread attention was the perfect harmony and good feeling which existed between the two.[11] There had been a time in the Father-

[10] The United Brethren, the Evangelical Association, the Dunkards.

[11] "Which fellowship has also been preserved sacred and inviolate, . . . so that one may well desire that such traces of harmony might also be found in Germany." (Life of Schlatter, p. 139.) Raynal, Burke, and others speak in high terms of the harmony existing between all the sects and churches of

land when jealousy had existed between them and when petty quarrels had divided them. The common sufferings and persecutions in more recent times had tended to smooth over their differences.[12] From the moment they arrived in Pennsylvania we see but little evidence of hostility. The members of both denominations being poor and dwelling in sparsely settled communities, they were unable to build separate churches, and in the majority of cases they founded Union churches,[13] in which they worshipped on alternate Sundays. In some cases this arrangement has been continued down to the present day.[14]

In view of this community of interest, members of one congregation often worshipped with the other, Lutherans and Reformed frequently intermarried, baptisms, marriages, and funerals

Pennsylvania,—overlooking, however, the numerous petty quarrels. Between the Moravians on the one side and the Lutherans and Reformed on the other there was a very strong feeling.

[12] "Bei aller Zerstückelung der Glaubensparteien haben die Pfälzer nach langen Kämpfen sich endlich vertragen gelernt." (Riehl, Pfälzer, p. 379.)

[13] Such a church had been built in the seventeenth century by Karl Ludwig in Mannheim, common to the three confessions and dedicated "zur heiligen Eintracht." (Riehl. Pfälzer, p. 386.)

[14] Some of these union churches are common to other denominations also ; such is Mellinger's meeting-house, in West Cocalico Township, Lancaster County, in which worship Lutherans, Reformed, Mennonites, and Dunkards.

were performed by ministers of either denomination, and, in general, lines of demarcation were very loosely drawn. Indeed, it would probably have been difficult for many of the people to say what were the essential differences between the Lutheran and Reformed churches, and a story is told of a man who said that the only difference was that the Lutherans said " Vater Unser," while the Reformed said " Unser Vater." All this dulled the edge of denominational feeling. It was easy to pass from one church to another, and throughout the eighteenth century Lutheranism was looked upon as closely allied to the Church of England,[15] while in a similar manner the Reformed Church was classed with the Presbyterians.[16]

A crying need of both churches before the fourth decade of the last century was the supply of regular ministers, of whom there were scarcely any, while the number of church members

[15] See p. 146, note.

[16] Thus in the constitution of the new Presbyterian church into which the Reformed church of Frankford (Philadelphia Co.) was merged we read: "And the said congregation being satisfied that the shade of difference between the principles of the German Reformed Church and those of the Presbyterians of the United States are scarcely discernible and unimportant," etc. (Dotterer, Hist. Notes, p. 27.) In colonial documents the Reformed are frequently spoken of as Dutch Presbyterians, or Calvinists.

amounted to many thousands. Often the school-master would read sermons and conduct services. There had been some distinguished men who in an unofficial way had tried to introduce some order; among the Reformed there were John Philip Boehm and George Michael Weiss, the former of whom founded the churches in Conestoga Valley and perhaps in Lancaster. The earliest Lutheran church was founded in Falkner's Swamp in 1720. The two Stoevers were especially active, and at every cross-road founded a Lutheran congregation and opened a church record; most of these churches still exist.[17]

It was not, however, till the fourth decade that official and systematic efforts were made to or-

[17] One of the early churches with which the name of John Caspar Stoever is connected is the well-known Reed church, in Tulpehocken, founded in 1727 by the settlers from Schoharie, N. Y. Like the cathedral of Durham, it was "half house of God, half castle" and served as a fort against the Indians. Mr. L. A. Wollenweber alludes to this double function in the following lines:

> "Do droben uf dem runde Berg,
>   Do steht die alte Riethe-Kerch;
>   Drin hot der Parre Stoever schon
>   Vor hunnert Jahr manch Predigt thun;
>   Gepredigt zu de arme, deitsche Leit
>   In seller, ach! so harten Zeit.
>   Auch wor die Kerch 'n gute Fort
>   Gegen der Indianer wilde Hort—
>   Un schliefen drin gar manch Nacht,
>   Die arme Settlers wo hen bewacht."

ganize the scattered congregations of Lutherans
and Reformed in Pennsylvania. Michael Schlatter, a native of St. Gall, Switzerland, came to
America in 1746 for the purpose of studying the
church situation, and of devising some means of
help. Through the aid of the Reformed Synod
of Holland, and the generous contribution of
friends in Germany, Holland, Switzerland, and
even England, he was enabled to bring over in
1752 six young men, regularly ordained ministers, and settled them in Philadelphia, Falkner's
Swamp, Lancaster, Reading, and other places.
Until 1792 the German Reformed Church in
Pennsylvania was under the general supervision
of the Holland Synod; since that date its affairs
have been administered by its own organization.[18]

Henry Melchior Muhlenberg occupies the
same relation to the Lutheran Church in Pennsylvania as Schlatter does to the Reformed. He
was a man of learning, energy, deep religious
feeling, and administrative talent. It is doubtful
if a better adapted man could have been found in
all Germany to undertake the peculiarly difficult
task he was called to do. The story of his life,
his travels, his labors, his tact in dealing with the

[18] At the end of the year 1899 there were 240,130 members
of the German Reformed Church in the United States.

difficult problems connected with the loose relations then prevailing among churches and sects,
—all these, as he relates them in his diary and in
the Hallesche Nachrichten,[19] must inspire every
reader with profound respect for this pioneer of
the Lutheran Church in America, and the father
of a distinguished line of preachers, warriors,
statesmen, and patriots.[20]

Through his efforts order was soon introduced
among the members of the Lutheran Church;
new congregations were started, and those already in existence were strengthened. The subsequent history of the Lutherans is different from
that of the Reformed Church, which to-day is almost entirely composed of the descendants of the
early Pennsylvania Germans, whereas the Lutherans have received exceedingly large additions
from the vast immigration from Germany in our
own century. In the country at large there are
many separate bodies of Lutherans,—the Penn-

[19] Muhlenberg came to Pennsylvania under the auspices of
the Orphan House founded at Halle by August Hermann
Francke, and for many years wrote back detailed accounts of
his labors, which, with the reports of other ministers, have
been published under the title of "Hallesche Nachrichten."
They are of extreme value for the student of the manners and
customs, the religious and social condition of the times.

[20] Among his descendants were General Peter Muhlenberg;
Frederick Augustus, Speaker of the House of Representatives;
William Augustus, founder of St. Johnland.

sylvania Germans being members of the " Ministerium of Pennsylvania and Adjacent States."

A problem of capital importance to both Reformed and Lutherans came into prominence
during the first decades of the nineteenth century and gradually assumed wide significance.
The question whether the services should be held
exclusively in German began to be agitated at
first in the larger cities, especially those where
the English influence was strong. As early as
1803, when the Rev. Henry A. Muhlenberg [21]
was called to Trinity Church in Reading, it was
understood that he should often preach in English. Evidently the time was not ripe for so
great a change, for we soon find the experiment
abandoned and German exclusively used. The
movement, however, could not be kept down;
the natural order of things brought it more and
more to the front, so that in many cases the result was the splitting up of congregations, one
part of which would continue to hold services
in German, while the other would introduce English.[22] The change, however, came slowly and
was stubbornly opposed by the conservative ele-

[21] Grandson of the patriarch Henry Melchior.
[22] Such was the origin of the St. Paul's Reformed Church in
Lancaster, built almost next door to the First Church; *English*
is used exclusively in both at the present time.

ment. It was undoubtedly owing to this conservatism that so many of the younger generation left and joined other churches. Feeling ran so high that the Reformed Synod of Frederick, Md., in 1826 publicly rebuked a young minister for giving an address in English.[23]

It is claimed that the Moravians are the oldest Protestant denomination in the world, dating back to the days of Huss. After the death of the great reformer, many of his followers continued in secret the worship of God according to their own doctrines, while openly professing to be members of the Catholic Church. Their secret heresy being discovered, they were forced to flee from their native land, and in 1722 settled in Saxony on the estate of Count Zinzendorf, where they founded the now historic town of Herrnhut. Zinzendorf, who was a Lutheran, became much interested in their peculiar views, and finally joined them and was made bishop. Missions from the beginning were one of the chief functions of the Moravians, and they already had sent missionaries to Greenland and other places before coming to America. It was natural, then, that they should cast their eyes to the heathen across the Atlantic. In 1735 a number of missionaries came to Georgia with the intention of

[23] Life of Philip Schaff, p. 153.

settling there and preaching the Gospel to the Indians; but the war with Spain interfered with their plans, and in 1740 they came to Pennsylvania, where they bought a large tract of land and founded Bethlehem.

In 1741 Zinzendorf came and took charge of the new settlement. He was inspired with the laudable desire to unite all the German Protestants in the colony, and organized, or rather took charge of, the movement already started, and which was known as the Pennsylvania Synod. John Gruber, Henry Antes, and John Bechtel had met in 1740 to talk over the unsettled condition of religion in Pennsylvania, and Antes advised a union of all German sects and denominations. On December 26, 1741, he published a circular inviting representatives of the different communions to attend a general meeting at Germantown, " not for the purpose of disputing, but in order to treat peaceably concerning the most important articles of faith and ascertain how far they might agree on the most essential points." A number of people met January 12, 1742, at the house of Theobald Endt, where the above-mentioned Pennsylvania Synod was organized. During the next ten months seven of these Synods were held in different places, at which Lutherans, Reformed, Schwenckfelders, Mennonites, Dunkards, and Separatists were present. The project failed through denominational jealousy. Bechtel, Antes, and others joined the Moravians, being attracted by Zinzendorf. It was the actions and success of the Moravians which hastened the coming of Schlatter and Muhlenberg, whose aim was to care for the long-neglected interests of the Reformed and Lutheran churches.[24]

The missionary efforts of the Moravians among the Indians greatly prospered; many converts were made and the settlements of Gnadenhütten, Friedenthal, and others were founded. The labors of such men as Post, Spangenberg, Nitschman, and Zeisberger, whom Thompson calls the " John Eliot of the West," present a picture of piety, self-denial, and patient endurance rarely equalled in the annals of missions. The French and Indian War with its intensified

---

[24] At one time the existence of the Lutheran Church in Lancaster was threatened by Nyberg, its pastor, who himself went over to the Moravians and wished to carry the congregation with him. The gentle Muhlenberg frequently indulges in harsh language concerning what he calls the machinations of the Moravians. No doubt Zinzendorf was ambitious and imperious ; John Wesley, who ardently admired him at first, came to see this later. (See Tyerman's Life of Wesley, vol. I. p. 207.) Yet the Moravians in Pennsylvania were inspired by true evangelical zeal ; Schaff calls them a "small but most lovely and thoroughly evangelical denomination."

race-hatred interfered with and practically put
an end to the mission-work on a large scale.

The doctrines of the Moravians were not very
different from those of the Lutherans;[25] they
were only marked by a greater depth of religious
feeling and the spirit of self-sacrifice. Their
manners and customs were peculiar to themselves and are picturesque and interesting. At
first the settlement at Bethlehem was communistic, but in 1760 a division of the property took place, the community retaining,
however, a tavern and a tanyard, 2000 acres
near Bethlehem and 5000 near Nazareth. The
profits on the property sold were devoted to the
cause of missions. In the olden times there was
a sharp distinction made not only between the
sexes, but between the different ages and conditions of the same sex. Each class had its own
place in church, often lived together, and had
its own peculiar festivals. The women were
outwardly marked by means of ribbons, children
wearing light-red, girls dark-red, the unmarried
sisters pink, the married women blue, and widows

[25] The Moravians do not indulge in the habit of dogmatiz-
ing, and refuse controversy. They have put forth no formu-
lated creed of their own, yet on the Continent they declare
their adhesion to the Augsburg Confession with its twenty-one
doctrinal articles. The great theme of their preaching is
Jesus Christ. (See Thompson, Moravian Missions, p. 9.)

white.[26] Even in death these distinctions were
kept up, and in the graveyard at Lititz the bodies
were buried according to age.[27] There was and
is still a deep touch of poetry over the religious
life of the Moravians. Not only were head and
heart cultivated in religion, but also the æsthetic
nature. This was largely done by means of
music, in which they excelled and which from
the earliest times they have cultivated. Music,
often very elaborate, marked all their services
and added a refining influence to the emotions
excited by religious worship. Bethlehem is still
thoroughly Moravian in many of its features, and
few towns in the United States offer more objects
of interest to the traveller than are to be seen
here in the way of schools, old buildings, church,
and graveyard.

The Roman Catholics had little influence in
provincial Pennsylvania. Although toward the
middle of last century their numbers were greatly
exaggerated, yet they were actually very small,
in 1757 being less than fourteen hundred in all. Of

[26] Henry, Sketches of Moravian Life. For description of
Moravian dress (with picture) see Ritter, p. 145.

[27] "No ornaments were allowed to disturb the simple uni-
formity of the tokens of remembrance ; the marble slab was
even limited in its length and breadth to 12 × 18 inches, and
these all flat on the grave-mound." (Ritter.) As late as
1820 an offer of $7500 for the privilege of a vault was refused.

the few German Catholics most afterwards became Protestants, and to-day it is rare to find a Catholic of Pennsylvania-German ancestry.

There is no more interesting or picturesque sect in the country, or indeed in the world, than the Mennonites. As they played so large a part in the first settlements of Pennsylvania, and as so many thousands of Americans are descended from them, it is worth while to devote a little space to their history.[28] To trace them to their origin we shall have to go back to the Waldenses of the twelfth and thirteenth centuries, and through them to the days of the primitive church. While the connection between the Mennonites and Waldenses is not absolutely proved historically, yet there is a fair argument made out by the supporters of this theory.[29] It is proved that in those places where the Mennonites, or Anabaptists, first arose there had been for long periods of time communities of Waldenses and related sects. The doctrines were the

[28] It is singular how little is known in this country of the Mennonites,—due undoubtedly to the desire and consistent effort on their part to be

> " little and unknown,
> Loved and prized by God alone."

[29] In recent years the arguments have been strongly summed up by Keller, Die Reformation und die älteren Reformparteien.

same: refusal to take oath, non-resistance, rejection of a paid ministry and infant baptism, simplicity of dress and life and of religious worship. In all these things the Mennonites are the logical if not the actual successors of the Waldenses.

If this historical connection were capable of proof, it would indeed be an inspiring thought, and one fraught with profound belief in the on-working of Providence, that through the Dark and the Middle Ages, in the days of ignorance, corruption, sin, tyranny, and persecution, the true Church of God, composed of those who worshipped Him in spirit and in truth, should be carried along, first openly, then in secret for long centuries, then finally, at the outbreak of the Reformation, once more boldly coming forth and proclaiming that true religion and undefiled consists not in form or ceremony, not in magnificent cathedrals built by man, but in the heart and in the life of the followers of the meek and lowly Jesus. The Mennonites, like the Waldenses, had no theology, cared not for intricate discussions of philosophy, but took the life of Christ and His teachings as their only rule of conduct. They did not believe in the union of Church and State, nor in putting pressure on any one in matters of religious belief; " Believe and let believe "

was their motto.[30] If any one could persuade
them out of the Bible, they were willing
to hear him; but neither persecution, fire,
sword, prison nor exile, could bend their wills,
or make them recant what they believed to be
the truth as it is in Christ Jesus. Not only were
they steadfast in the faith, but they rejoiced in
dying the death of martyrs.[31]

The Mennonites have often been confused
with the Anabaptists of the Münster rebellion,

[30] Their attitude in this respect was almost identical with
that of John Wesley, who once made the remark, "As to all
opinions that do not strike at the root of Christ we think and
let think."

[31] Salat in his "Chronika" says of the Mennonites : "Mit
fröhlicher, lächelnder Gebärde heischten, wünschten und be-
gehrten sie den Tod, nahmen ihn ganz begierig an und gingen
ihn ein mit Absingung deutscher Psalmen und anderer Ora-
tionen." (Quoted by Nitsche, Gesch. der Wiedertäufer in der
Schweiz, p. 35.) The death of Felix Manz, January 5, 1527,
is so inspiring that I cannot forbear quoting the description of
it given in Brons' Ursprung, etc., der Taufgesinnten oder Mennoniten (p. 40): "As he stood there [on the boat], beneath him
the waters of Lake Zürich, above him the blue sky, and round
about him the giant mountains with their snow-capped sum-
mits lighted up by the sun, his soul, in the presence of death,
rose above all these things. And as on one side a minister
urged him to recant, he scarcely heard him ; but when, on the
other side, he heard the voice of his mother, and when his
brothers besought him to remain steadfast, he sang, while his
hands were being bound, with a loud voice, 'In manus tuas
Domine commendo spiritum meum,' and immediately afterwards he sank beneath the waves."

yet Menno himself wrote a book against these fanatics, and the only connection between the two parties was that both were called Anabaptists, then a term of reproach. The vast majority of those who are now known as Mennonites [32] were earnest, sensible, intelligent, God-fearing, industrious, upright men and women.[33] Many of their doctrines were simply two or three hundred years ahead of the times, and the last decade of the nineteenth century has seen their main doctrines universally admitted. They believed war to be unchristian: the Peace Congress at the Hague shows at least how widespread is the desire to abolish armed conflicts. They believed in the separation of Church and State: the Constitution of our own country is based on that principle. They believed in freedom of conscience: to-day this is practised in all civilized countries. Although quaint and curious, and in some respects narrow even to-day, yet they deserve the credit of being the torch-bearers of religious liberty.

The first colony of Mennonites in Pennsyl-

[32] So called from Menno, Simon born in Witmarsum, Friesland, in 1492. He was to the moderate part of the Anabaptists what Luther and Zwingli were to the churches founded by them.

[33] See the testimonies to this effect collected by Arnold, Kirchen- und Ketzergeschichte.

vania was that at Germantown; the great resemblance between them and the Quakers made
the latter welcome them and they often worshipped together. It was to the monthly meeting at Rigert Worrell's that Pastorius, Hendricks, and the Op den Graeff brothers presented
the famous petition against slavery in 1688, the
first instance of the kind in America. It is an interesting fact that the Dutch Mennonites (like
the Huguenots) were in the main artisans, and
especially weavers; and no sooner had Germantown been settled than they began to make
cloth and linen, which almost immediately won
for itself a widespread reputation.

While there were Mennonites settled in other
parts of Pennsylvania, Lancaster County was
and is still their chief centre. They were expert
farmers and soon prospered; to-day the best
farms, the stateliest barns, and the sleekest cattle belong to them. In general they have retained the manners and customs of their fathers;
many still dress in quaint garb, the women wearing caps even in their housework.[34] They wor-

[34] We have an interesting glimpse of the appearance of the
Swiss Mennonites shortly before coming to Pennsylvania : "Es
war ein ganz hartes Volk von Natur, das Ungemach ertragen
konnte, mit langen, ungeschorenen Bärten, mit unordentlicher
Kleidung, schweren Schuhen, die mit Hufeisen und grossen

ship in plain meeting-houses, choose their ministers by lot, will not take oath, nor bear arms. In certain localities, such as Strasburg and Landisville, they outnumber all other denominations.

Yet while all this is true, those families which have moved to the city or gone to other States have gradually left the old-fashioned faith of their fathers and become worldly. Some interesting facts in this connection could be given.[35] Yet the sect is still large; in 1883 they had in Lancaster County 3500 members, 41 meeting-houses, and 47 ministers, 8 of whom were bishops.[36]

Like all denominations, large or small, the

Nägeln sehr schwer beschlagen waren. Sie waren sehr eifrig Gott zu dienen mit Gebet, Lesen und Anderem, waren sehr einfach in all ihrem Thun wie Lämmer und Tauben. . . . Denn davon, dass sie in der Schweiz auf dem Gebirge gewohnt hatten, ferne von Dörfern und Städten, und wenig mit andern Menschen Umgang gehabt hatten, ist ihre Sprache ganz plump und ungebildet." (Müller, p. 271.)

[35] Take the family of Heinrich Pannebecker, one of the Mennonite settlers of Germantown. In spite of his own principles of non-resistance, 125 of his descendants took part in the Civil War. When, a short time ago, Judge Brubaker of Lancaster died, his place was immediately occupied by Judge Landis; both were descendants of the Swiss Mennonites of Lancaster County, one of whose principles was not to take oath. It may be of interest to add that H. C. Frick, Mr. Carnegie's partner, is also a descendant of the Swiss Mennonites.

[36] The latest statistics give 57,948 as the total membership of all branches of the Mennonites in the country.

Mennonites had their schisms; even in the life-
time of Menno Simon a council was held at
Dort in 1632 to settle on terms of agreement.
One of the most important divisions occurred in
Switzerland, and resulted in the formation of a
sub-sect, which later was transferred to the Palatinate (where it still exists), and thence to Pennsylvania. This was the branch known as the
Amish, founded by Jacob Ammen of Canton
Berne, his purpose being to preserve more severity and simplicity of doctrine and dress. The
use of buttons was considered worldly vanity,
and only hooks and eyes were allowed on the
clothing.[37] The Amish still exist in Pennsylvania, where they worship in private houses, having no regular minister, and adhering rigidly to
the confession adopted by the Synod of Dort in
1632.[38]

But even in the New World the tendency to
schism showed itself. The Reformed Mennonites
were founded by Francis Herr toward the end of
the eighteenth century. Having withdrawn from
the regular body, he held meetings in his own
house, and drew many people to him. His son,

[37] Hence called "Häftler or Hookers." (See Müller, Bernische Täufer, p. 314 ff.)
[38] There are to-day 12,876 Amish and 2,438 Old Amish in
the United States, making a total of 15,314.

John Herr, carried on the work and became bishop of the little sect, together with Abraham Landis and Abraham Groff.[39]

The River Brethren were founded by Jacob Engel, who came in his childhood from Switzerland, and lived in Conestoga Township. He was a Mennonite and became convinced that this sect as it then was lacked religious vitality; and in connection with his brother John and several others he established a system of stated prayer-meetings. The little flock soon increased, ministers were appointed, and meetings held in Engel's house. They had no design at first to found a separate sect, but, as almost always happens, the logic of circumstances forced them to this, and in 1776 a religious organization was made. They are commonly supposed to be a branch of the Dunkards, but are rather an offshoot of the Mennonites. They took their name from the fact that they originated near the Susquehanna. They are strictly non-resistant and elect their bishop by general vote.

The Dunkards, now a flourishing denomination, were founded by Alexander Mack of Schwarzenau in Westphalia in 1708, though their real origin dates from 1719, when about

[39] See Musser's Reformed Mennonite Church.

twenty families came to Pennsylvania and settled in Germantown, Skippack (Montgomery Co.), Oley (Berks), and on the Conestoga Creek (Lancaster Co.). Their leader was Peter Baker, who had been a minister under Mack in Sehwarzenau. In 1723 Baker made a missionary tour through the German settlements and established a church at Conestoga,[40] consisting of thirty-six members. In 1724 Conrad Beissel was chosen assistant to Baker, "but Beissel, being wise in his own conceit, soon caused trouble in the church in regard to the Sabbath," he declaring that this should be celebrated on the seventh day. The result was that when in 1729 Alexander Mack himself came to Pennsylvania, the question was put to the Conestoga church, and being decided against Beissel by a large majority, he with a few others withdrew and organized at Ephrata a society of Seventh-Day Baptists. The Conestoga church at its organization had settlements in the present counties of Lancaster, Berks, Dauphin, and Lebanon, over which Baker had charge till the arrival of Mack, who then assumed the office of bishop, with Baker as assistant. The latter died in 1734, Mack in 1735.

[40] Lancaster County was not formed till 1729 ; till that year it was known as Conestoga.

Settlements were made later in Virginia and especially in Ohio, where the Dunkards are still numerous.[41] Their doctrines are not very different from those of the Mennonites; like them they disbelieve in infant baptism, refuse to take oath or to bear arms. They differ from them in the mode of baptizing, which they perform by dipping (*tunken*), hence the name of Tunker or Dunkard.

Perhaps the most interesting phenomenon of religious life in early Pennsylvania was the rise and progress of the German Seventh-Day Baptists and the establishment of the monastic community at Ephrata, in Lancaster County.

We have seen that Beissel with a few others left the Conestoga church and came to Cocalico Creek, where they settled down. Beissel was a man of unusual abilities, though of only limited education. He was born in 1690 at Eberbach in the Palatinate, where his father was a baker, a trade which he followed himself. Being converted to pietism, however, he came to Pennsylvania in 1720, intending to spend his life in solitary communion with God. After leaving the Conestoga church he lived for a time the life of

---

[41] There are in all 108,694 Dunkards, divided into Conservatives, Old Order, Progressive, and German Seventh-Day Baptists, the latter of whom amount to only 194.

a hermit on the Cocalico, surrounded by many who built themselves cottages and imitated his ascetic life. Among those whom he thus attracted was a German Reformed minister of Tulpehocken, John Peter Miller, and Conrad Weiser, a Lutherän (who afterwards left), and later some of the leaders of the Dunkards, Kalklöser, Valentine Mack, and John Hildebrand.

As the numbers increased it became necessary to provide accommodations for them, and in 1735 a convent for sisters was erected called Kedar; in 1738 a corresponding monastery for the brethren, and later many other buildings were built. [42] In 1740 there were thirty-six single brethren and thirty-five sisters. At one time the society, including the married members, amounted to nearly three hundred. The ruler or prior of this community, Conrad Beissel,—called by his followers Gottrecht Friedsam,—seems to have been a man of great personal magnetism and drew the loyal affection of all who met him. He was looked on with mystic affection and even wor-

[42] A number of these old buildings are still standing, and the curious visitor can see the rooms in which the inmates lived, the chapel in which they worshipped, and even the very sacramental utensils which they used one hundred and fifty years ago. Interesting descriptions of Ephrata have been given by Seidensticker and Sachse.

ship, some going so far as to regard him as a second Christ.[43]

It would be a pleasant task to give a detailed account of this strange community, its poetic customs, its midnight religious services, often lasting till daybreak, its weird music, its exaggerated mystic piety, its monastic garb and cloister names;[44] but all this would lead us too far. The community gradually died out, until at present only a small remnant remains, who still meet however, from time to time, and worship in the manner of their ancestors.

Still another interesting sect is that of the Schwenckfelders, so named after Casper von Schwenckfeld of Ossing in Silesia, who was a

[43] This was the evident meaning of a verse in one of the hymns which Sauer published for Beissel :

> " Sehet, sehet, sehet an,
> Sehet, sehet an den Mann !
> Der von Gott erhöhet ist,
> Der ist unser Herr und Christ,"

and which was the cause of a quarrel between the two. (See Penn. Mag., vol. XII.)

[44] Some of these names were genuinely poetical, such as Sisters Genoveva, Eusebia, Petronella, Blandina, Euphrosina, Zenobia. Whittier, who alone of American poets has felt the poetry of Pennsylvania-German life, has a Hymn of the Dunkards, beginning :

> " Wake, sisters, wake, the day-star shines ;
> Above Ephrata's eastern pines
> The day is breaking cool and calm.
> Wake, sisters, wake to prayer and psalm."

contemporary of Luther, and who incurred the wrath of the latter, because of his peculiar tenets, chiefly concerning the Eucharist, the efficacy of the divine Word, the human nature of Christ, and infant baptism. On account of the latter his followers were frequently confused with the Anabaptists. Many clergymen and nobles in Silesia and elsewhere espoused his doctrines, especially in Liegnitz and Jauer, where almost the whole population were his adherents. Later they were persecuted first by the Lutherans, then by the Jesuit missionaries sent to convert them in 1719. In these troubles only one thing was left them—flight. In 1726 more than one hundred and seventy families escaped from Harpersdorf, Armenruh, and Hockenau, and making their way on foot to Upper Lusatia, then a part of Saxony, found shelter near Greisenberg, Görlitz, Hennersdorf, Berthelsdorf, and Herrnhut, where they were hospitably received by Zinzendorf and the Senate of Görlitz. They lived in Saxony eight years, but in 1734 were forced once more to take up the life of exiles. In 1732 two families went to Pennsylvania, and their report and the advice of certain benefactors in Holland induced forty families to follow. They arrived September 24, 1734, in Philadelphia, where some settled, while others went to Montgomery, Berks,

and Lehigh counties. They now form two congregations, with three hundred families and five
churches or schoolhouses.[45]

We have already discussed the strong pietistic
tendency in Pennsylvania, and how it manifested
itself not only in the sects, but among the regular
confessions. This deep, personal religion was
especially cultivated by the Moravians. It is
well known that John Wesley was first brought
to a sense of the defects of a mere formal or-
thodoxy and the need of a heart-religion through
the Moravians. On his journey to Georgia, he
came into close contact with David Nitschman,
and, after landing, with Spangenberg, and learnt
from them the power of God as manifested in the
heart. It was through Peter Boehler in London
that he finally became convinced of the possibility of a saving faith, instant conversion, and the
joy and peace of believing.[46] This early connection with German emotional religion had far-
reaching consequences. It is a singular fact
that Methodism in America was founded by Ger-

[45] Among the well-known Schwenckfelder names are Wieg-
ner, Kriebel, Jäckel (Yeakel), Hübner, Heydrich, Anders.
Hartranft, Schultze, Weiss, Meschter.

[46] See Tyerman's Life of Wesley: also Wesley's Journal. In
1738 he spent nearly two weeks in Herrnhut. He writes: "I
would gladly spend my life here. Oh, when shall this Chris-
tianity cover the earth, as the waters cover the sea?"

mans who had been converted by Wesley, who himself had received from the Moravians some of his peculiar doctrines—doctrines which he in turn passed on to his fellow countrymen and which were destined to exert so extraordinary an influence on the religious life of the New World.

We have seen that of the Palatines who over-ran London in 1709, some three thousand were sent to Ireland. In 1756 Wesley visited the town of Ballygarrane and preached to the Germans, of whom he says in his Journal: [47] " They retain much of the temper and manners of their own country, having no resemblance to those among whom they live. I found much life among this plain, artless, serious people. The whole town came together in the evening, and praised God for the consolation." Of this number were Barbara Heck and Philip Embury, who, on account of difficulties in the way of getting a living in Ireland, with many others came to New York. This was in 1760, and six years later Philip Embury held the first Methodist meeting in this country, in the historic sail-loft in John Street.[48]

Methodism was introduced into Pennsylvania a little later by Captain Webb, one of Embury's

[47] June 16, 1756.
[48] Buckley, Hist. of Methodists in the United States, p. 101.

assistants.[49]   Among those who welcomed it was
Martin Boehm of Lancaster County, who had
been a Mennonite and later was one of the
founders of the United Brethren.   The Boehm
homestead became a centre of Methodist influence in Pennsylvania.   Asbury frequently
stopped here, many powerful revivals were held,
numbers of the German and Swiss farmers in the
neighborhood were converted, most famous of
all being Father Henry Boehm,—son of Martin,—who was Asbury's travelling-companion
for many years.   Methodism spread more slowly
through the cities, and it was only after the beginning of the present century that churches
were founded in Lancaster, Reading, and other
cities.   To-day a large proportion of the members
and ministers in the State are of Pennsylvania-
German descent.[50]

This, however, is not the only way in which
Methodism has influenced the German inhabitants of the commonwealth.   Although it is denied that the United Brethren Church was

[49] See Penn. Mag., vol. XII.   It is a little curious that in
Philadelphia as well as in New York the first Methodist meeting was held in a sail-loft.

[50] Among the bishops are Bowman, Hartzell, and Keener
(Church South).   A glance at the minutes of the Pennsylvania
conferences will show how large a percentage of the ministers
are of Pennsylvania-German descent.

founded in imitation of Methodism, yet the latter certainly exerted a vast deal of influence on the former. The two founders of this denomination were Martin Boehm and Philip William Otterbein, the former a Mennonite, the latter a peculiarly spiritually-minded Reformed minister. Both Boehm and Otterbein experienced conversion, in the genuine Methodistic sense of that word, and both, moved by the Spirit, began to preach a heart-religion. Great success attended their efforts, and thousands crowded their revival services. In 1768,[51] at one of these meetings, they met for the first time, and falling on each other's neck cried out, " Wir sind Brüder." Some years after a regular church organization was formed, and received from the above incident the name of United Brethren. For many years there was a close fraternal relation between the newly founded church and the Methodists; they adopted many features of the Discipline, had class- and prayer-meetings, the itinerant system, annual and general conferences, and other details. For many years fraternal delegates were sent to the respective conferences, and letters were written bearing friendly greetings. Otterbein was the intimate friend of Asbury, and it

[51] The date is not sure. See Berger, Hist. of the United Brethren, p. 78.

was on the advice of the latter that he went to Baltimore, to the German Reformed Church, which later became the first church of the United Brethren.

It seemed to be the policy of Methodism in its early years in America to discourage all evangelical work carried on in other languages than English,—apparently because the authorities were convinced that all others would soon die out. Hence they welcomed the efforts made by the United Brethren in evangelistic work among the Germans, and consequently both were on friendly terms and without denominational jealousy. Some indeed did desire a union and propositions were made looking toward this end. Nothing came of them, however, and after some years both denominations ceased sending delegates and friendly messages to the respective conferences.

The United Brethren Church was originally almost exclusively composed of Pennsylvania Germans and is now largely made up of their descendants.[52]

Still more closely connected with Methodism is the Evangelical Association, founded by Jacob Albright, who had been brought up a Lutheran,

---

[52] 264,980 members in all.

and who in 1796, "yearning for the salvation
of his spiritually neglected German-speaking
brethren, started out as a humble layman to
preach to them the Gospel of Christ. His labors
extended over large portions of Pennsylvania
and into parts of Maryland and Virginia and resulted in the saving of many souls."[53] Albright
had originally no thought of founding a new religious organization, but finally, in 1800, he
yielded to the oft-repeated and urgent requests of
those whom he had led to the Lord and began
the work of organization. Their Discipline,
largely taken from that of the Methodists, was
published in 1809. A glance therein will show
how thorough the influence of the latter Church
was:—they have quarterly, annual, and general
conferences; bishops, presiding elders, the itine-
rancy, class-meetings, and other Methodist characteristics.[54]

[53] See Discipline of the United *E*vangelical Church.

[54] Albright had little knowledge of *E*nglish and preached in
German to the people of *E*astern Pennsylvania. If Asbury
had cared to form a German ministry within Methodism, this
separate body of German Methodists probably would not have
been formed. The original conference in 1807 called itself
the 'Newly formed Methodist Conference.' Albright had
been a Methodist, and was such still in his heart, faith, and
practice. (See Berger, Hist. of the United Brethren in Christ,
p. 193.) In 1899 there were 117,613 members in the *E*vangelical Association.

The spirit of schism which seems ever present in religious bodies, manifested itself in the Evangelical Association. Some dozen or fifteen years ago, certain questions arose concerning the General Conference and especially the episcopacy, and gradually the differences of opinion grew so widespread, that in 1891 two General Conferences were held each claiming to be the legal representative of the Church. Hence arose the body known as the United Evangelical Church, the first General Conference of which was held in 1894. In their Discipline no changes were made in the accepted doctrines of the Church, but several new articles were added and the language of all was changed.[55]

Another body of Christians widely spread in Pennsylvania is the Church of God, sometimes called Winebrennerians from the founder, John Winebrenner. He was a minister of the Reformed Church, and settled in Harrisburg in 1820, where a revival soon broke out under his preaching. This being regarded as an innovation in the customs of the Reformed Church, Winebrenner met so strong an opposition that the doors of his church were closed against him, and about the year 1825 he was forced to sepa-

[55] The United *Evangelical* Church now has 59,830 members.

rate from his denomination. His preaching was heard by great numbers of Germans, and in 1829 a regular organization was established. Owing to their doctrine of immersion they are classed with the Baptists. The polity of the Church of God, however, is Methodistic in some respects; the Annual Eldership corresponds to the Annual Conference, and the General Eldership to the General Conference.[56]

We have only space here for a word or two on the influence of other English denominations on the Pennsylvania Germans. In many cases the Presbyterian, Episcopalian, Baptist, and Swedenborgian churches, especially in large cities, are swelled in numbers by the descendants of these people.

[56] The membership amounts at present to 38,000.

CHAPTER VII.

IN PEACE AND IN WAR.

MR. FISKE has estimated that the 20,000 English who settled in New England before 1640 have increased to fifteen millions. Considering the large families of the old-fashioned Pennsylvania Germans it would seem probable that the 100,000 or more who came over before 1775 have multiplied at least as rapidly as their Puritan neighbors. It would be a moderate statement, then, to say that to-day there are between four and five million people in the United States who in some line or other can trace their ancestry to the early German and Swiss settlers of Pennsylvania. Of these not far from two million still inhabit the State founded by their ancestors. This mass of people must have had more or less influence on the development of the United States, and they themselves must have been largely moulded by their new surroundings. As Freytag says, " In dem unaufhörlichen Einwirken des Einzelnen auf das Volk und des Volkes auf

den Einzelnen läuft das Leben einer Nation." [1]
In the present chapter we shall endeavor to
show some of the ways in which this mutual influence manifests itself; how the people have met
the new conditions in which they were placed;
what has been their attitude to the State in politics and in the various wars through which the
country has passed since they came; in short, to
tell, in brief outline, the share that the Germans
have had in the development of Pennsylvania in
particular and the United States in general.

In regard to politics we are struck by the fact
that the Pennsylvania Germans have not stamped
themselves so strongly on the country as their
numbers would warrant. Great statesmen and
men of national reputation are not numerous—
not so much so proportionately, for instance,
as in the case of Huguenots and Scotch-Irish.
In Pennsylvania down to the middle of the
eighteenth century the public offices were almost
entirely in the hands of English-speaking people.
In'the city of Lancaster the office of burgess had
always been held by an Englishman till 1750,

[1] Freytag, vol. IV. p. I. Cf. also, "von solchem Stand-
punkte verläuft das Leben einer Nation in einer unaufhör-
lichen Wechselwirkung des Ganzen auf den Einzelnen und des
Mannes auf das Ganze. Jedes Menschenleben, auch das
Kleine, giebt einen Theil seines Inhalts ab an die Nation."
(*Ibid.*, vol I, p. 24.)

when Dr. Adam S. Kuhn was elected.[2]   From
that time, however, the German element is more
and more represented, and since the Revolution
their proportion of local officers in the towns and
cities of Berks, Lancaster, and the other counties
has been very large.[3]   Up to the Revolution,
however, the political activity of the Germans
was largely confined to local affairs.   Nor is this
to be wondered at.   Hitherto they had formed a
compact body of their own, pre-eminently a rural
population, whose chief occupation was to found
homes for themselves and children in the New
World.   Then, too, they had come from a land
where there was little chance for political activity, where the government was despotic, and
where the country-folk had little or no voice in
the affairs of state.   This is true not only of the

[2] The Lutheran pastor in Lancaster, Rev. Joh. Fr. Handschuh, gives expression to his joy over this event in his diary:
"Den 20. Sept. kamen einige Kirchenräthe und erzählten mir
mit Bewegung und Freude ihres Herzens, wie . . . unsern
Kirchenrath Dr. Adam Kuhn hätte man zum Oberbürger-
meister . . . erwählet." (Hall. Nach., I. p. 542.)   At the
same time Jacob Schlauch, also a Lutheran, was elected
Unterbürgermeister, while of four other Lutherans elected one
was High Constable, and three others were assessors.

[3] For instance, in Reading all the chief burgesses (ten in
number) and twelve of the seventeen mayors have been German (1883); a similar proportion prevails for justices of peace,
aldermen, etc.   In the borough of Kutztown all the burgesses
except one have been German.

Palatinate and Würtemberg, but also of Switzerland, for even in that land of freedom, the proto-
type of our own land, the peasantry had no
political rights whatever until nearly one hundred
years after the emigration to Pennsylvania began.[4] It must also be remembered that a considerable number of the people, Dunkards, Mennonites, and Moravians, refused on religious
grounds to hold political office.[5]

Can we wonder then that the Germans of
Pennsylvania were a long time in coming to an
active and enthusiastic exercise of their privileges
in the matter of political intrigues and office-
holding? We do not mean to say that they were
all indifferent to the political questions of the
day, or that they had no interest in public affairs,
but only that in the eighteenth century, at least,

[4] "Die Bewohner der Landschaften waren bis *Ende* des
achtzehnten Jahrhunderts thatsächlich von der Staatsleitung
ausgeschlossen." (Dändliker, II. p. 632.) Freytag, speaking
of the Thirty Years' War, says: "Noch hundert Jahre sollten
die Nachkommen der Überlebenden die männlichste Empfin-
dung entbehren, politische Begeisterung." (Vol. III. p. 13.)

[5] Germantown was incorporated as a borough town in 1689,
but about 1704 lost its charter because no one was willing to
accept the various offices. The records of this short-lived
municipality read like an extract from "Diedrich Knicker-
bocker." In 1795 the Moravian Bishop Ettwein deplored the
dereliction of "some of the brethren in Lancaster who had
joined a political body called the Democrats and even accepted
office therein." (Ritter, p. 98.)

eagerness for office was not a marked trait of their character.

Since the Revolution, however, they have been more and more prominent in State and county politics. Dr. Egle says that in the Constitutional Convention of 1789–90 it was their votes that insured the passage of the new Constitution. Not only was the local magistracy largely drawn from their ranks,[6] but in the larger field of State politics they have furnished a number of distinguished men. The names of Kuhl, Antes, Muhlenberg, Hiester, Graff, etc., are familiar to the student of early Pennsylvania history, while no fewer than nine of the governors of the commonwealth were of German descent.[7] It was Governor George Wolf who finally introduced the public-school system, and Joseph Ritner's manly protest against the usurpations of the slave States called forth from Whittier a tribute to the sturdiness of Pennsylvania-German character.[8]

[6] In 1777 all but one of the officers of Lancaster were Germans.

[7] Snyder, Hiester, Schulze, Wolf, Ritner, Shunk, Hartranft, Bigler, Beaver. In this connection may be mentioned Governors Bouck of New York, Ramsey of Minnesota,—Lebanon County German on the maternal side,—Schley of Georgia, John Bigler of California, and Geo. L. Shoup of Idaho.

[8] " Thank God for the token ! one lip is still free,
   One spirit untrammelled, unbending one knee," etc.
                                        (Works, vol. III. p. 47.)

In national politics their prominence is not so apparent, since here they come in competition with all the rest of the country. Yet we must record the names of Frederick A. Muhlenberg, president of the convention which ratified the Constitution of the United States,[9] Michael Hillegass, Treasurer of the Continental Congress, and such men as Simon Cameron, Colonel John W. Forney, John Wanamaker, and others. Of course it would be inappropriate here to give a catalogue of men in public life, or even a statistical view of the same. Yet I have carefully gone over the files of the *Congressional Record* from its first issue down to the present, and find in every Congress from five to ten typical Pennsylvania-German names, representing the Keystone State at Washington;[10] other States, especially in the West, have often been represented by men who trace their origin to the early German settlements of Pennsylvania.

[9] He was also first Speaker of the House of Representatives under Washington's administration.

[10] Among these names are Hiester, Muhlenberg, Krebs, Wolf, Bucher, Wagener, Fry, Hubley, Sheffer, Keim, Yost, Ritter, Frick, Erdman, Leib, Strohm, Everhart, Kuhns, Trout, Kurtz, Kunkel, Leidy, Longnecker, Lehman, Coffroth, Glassbrenner, Koontz, Haldeman, Albright, Negley, Shoemaker, Shellenberger, Yocum, Klotz, Beltzhoover, Ermentrout. In Berks County out of twenty United States congressmen from 1789–1885, fifteen were of German descent.

Such is a brief glance at the public life of Pennsylvania Germans in politics and in times of
peace. It remains to give a similar brief view of
their services in the various wars through which
the country has passed during the last two centuries. Here it may be stated without fear of
contradiction that they have shown themselves as
ready as any of their fellow countrymen to sac-
rifice life and fortune for their country's good.

When the Germans began to come to Pennsylvania the troubles with the Indians in New England and New York were over. In the former
colony the terrible prowess of the Puritan warriors had crushed the Pequots and Narragansetts;
in New York the wise conduct of the Dutch and
English had permanently attached the Five Nations to the interests of England, in spite of all
the intrigues of the French to win them over.

The attitude of Pennsylvania toward the Indians from the first had been one of conciliation
and kindness; the example set by Penn, of dealing with them with strict honesty, had been in
general followed by his successors. The relations between the Germans and the Indians had
always been friendly, and the former had shown
a deep interest in the spiritual welfare of the latter. As early as 1694 Kelpius declared his desire to preach the Gospel to them, while the

Indian missions of the Moravians form one of the noblest chapters of State history.

For many years Pennsylvania was entirely free from the dread and terror that had been the inseparable companion of the early settlers of New England. The Delawares, who occupied that part of the country before the coming of Penn, gradually and peaceably receded before the onward march of white settlers, till about the middle of the century they had retired beyond the Blue Mountains and left practically all the territory to the east and south to the whites.

Soon after, however, this state of affairs came to an end. Dissatisfaction and discontent,— largely on account of the famous " Walking Purchase,"—the intrigues of the French, and especially the disastrous defeat of Braddock in 1755, let loose upon the frontier settlements of Pennsylvania all the horrors of Indian warfare. Among the greatest sufferers were the German settlers, especially in Berks and Northampton counties. Hundreds were slain and scalped, houses, barns, and crops went up in flames, children and women were carried into captivity. The letters of Conrad Weiser, Muhlenberg, and others give many harrowing details of scenes which were then of almost daily occurrence.[11]

[11] Some of these descriptions are very dramatic,—such as

The attitude of the Germans was at first somewhat indifferent, owing chiefly to the non-combatant doctrines of Mennonites and Moravians, and to the fact that in politics they in general followed the lead of the Quakers. Yet when the danger became more acute many offered their lives in the service of the commonwealth. Franklin says: "Much unanimity prevailed in all ranks; eight hundred persons signed at the outset. The Dutch were as hearty in this measure as the English, and one entire company was formed of Dutch." [12]

that of the man with his two daughters, who had loaded their wagon and were prepared to escape the next day, and the preceding night the girls, being "angst und bange ums Herz, sie sagten zum Vater es wäre ihnen so traurig zu Muthe, als ob sie bald sterben sollten, und verlangten das Lied zu singen: 'Wer weiss, wie nahe mir mein Ende,' etc., sungen es auch mit einander vom Anfange bis ans Ende, thaten ihr Abendgebet, und legten sich zur Ruhe." The next day the Indians came and both the girls were killed. (See Muhlenberg, in Hall. Nach., vol. II. p. 465.)

[12] Watson, p. 273. Cf. also letter of Daniel Dulaney (Penn. Mag., vol. III. p. 11 ff.): "The Germans complained that no measures had been taken to avert the calamity, . . . demanded arms, . . . and signed an application for a militia law." It was not strange that they should be willing thus to fight to save their homes. Many had been soldiers in Germany and Switzerland. In the forces mustered in Albany in 1711 to be sent to Canada, one thousand were Palatines. (Gordon, p. 163.) Out of a whole population of 356 Palatines in Queensbury, N. Y., 40 men joined the expedition against

As to actual numbers engaged in hostilities it is hard to give complete figures. In the Pennsylvania Archives we find a list of provincial officers in 1754; out of 33, 8 are German. In 1756, in Conrad Weiser's battalion, 22 out of 38 are German. The rolls of privates are not given, but we have other reasons for believing that they were practically all of the same nationality. Thus a German chaplain was appointed; Gordon says (p. 342) that Weiser's battalion consisted of Germans, and in the list of Captain Nicholas Wetterholt's regiment every name is German. Even in the other two battalions many Germans were enlisted.

So much for actual warfare. The services of the Germans in other respects are just as important. Most distinguished of all was Conrad Weiser, who for many years was the official Indian interpreter and agent of Pennsylvania. Before the war he did all he could to pacify the Indians; he was frequently sent by the government to them, and successfully carried out many dangerous missions. When war broke out he raised a battalion and was everywhere active. His name occurs in these events more frequently

Canada; and in Amesbury 52 volunteered out of a total population of 250. (See *O'Callaghan, Doc. Hist. of N. Y.*, vol. III. pp. 571, 2.)

than that of almost any other at this time,—he was constantly making reports, indorsing petitions, explaining the condition of the inhabitants, giving orders and suggestions. It was he more than any other man who kept the Five Nations faithful to the English at that time. The value of that service can hardly be overestimated.[13] The spirit of this heroic man may be seen in the following words written by him to Richard Peters, October 4, 1757: "I think meselfe unhappy; to fly with my family I can't do. I must stay if they all go." [14]

In the very forefront of the French and Indian War were the Moravians. No group of people suffered more, did more service, or showed more heroism than these messengers of the gospel of peace. At the first mutterings of war they became objects of suspicion to their fellow countrymen. Their intimate relations with the Indians, their settlements at Gnadenhütten and elsewhere, their frequent journeys through the wilderness, often extending as far as New York,—all this tended to raise suspicions. Then, too, their peculiar customs, their early communistic life,

[13] Weiser says himself that the council of the Six Nations always looked on him as a friend and as one of their own nation. (See Penn. Arch., 1st Series, vol. I. p. 672.)

[14] Penn. Arch., 1st Ser., vol. III. p. 283.

elaborate ritual, and peculiar dress seemed especially to the Scotch-Irish Presbyterians to smack of Romanism. We have already seen how the fear of the Catholics, together with politics, had led to the establishment of English schools for the Germans. The suspicion of the Moravians is only another symptom of the same fear. Even the French themselves seemed to believe that the Moravians would go over to their side whenever they should approach. This suspicion was unfounded, and the whole country awoke from their error when, on November 24, 1756, the massacre of Gnadenhütten occurred, in which not only the Indian converts, but Martin Nitschman, his wife, and several other Moravians perished.

Although non-combatants, the Moravians were reasonable; they fortified Bethlehem, brought together a large quantity of provisions, and even armed themselves in case of last extremity; in many ways they were of invaluable assistance to the cause.[15] Their heroism was manifest in word and deed. "The country,"

[15] In 1755 Timothy Horsfield writes: "At moderate computation the Brethren have lost £1500, and the expense they are daily at in victualling the people, with their horses, who pass and repass through Bethlehem, and supply them with powder and ball.' (Penn. Arch., 1st Series, vol. II. p. 523.)

wrote Spangenberg to Zinzendorf, "is full of fear and tribulation. In our churches there is light. We live in peace and feel the presence of the Saviour." The 8th of September, 1755, which witnessed the defeat of Count Dieskau, was distinguished at Bethlehem "by an enthusiastic missionary conference, composed of four bishops, sixteen missionaries, and eighteen female assistants, who covenanted anew to be faithful to the Lord, and to press forward into the Indian country as long as it was possible, in spite of wars and rumors of wars." [16]

The services in general of the Moravians to the country were great. Missionaries like Spangenberg and Post were of the utmost value in keeping the Indians quiet for many years, and many important embassies were intrusted to their care.[17]

[16] De Schweinitz, Life of Zeisberger, p. 222.

[17] "During the late bloody war, all commerce between the white people and *I*ndians being suspended, he [Post] was intrusted first by this government, and then by Brig.-Gen. Forbes, with negotiations to secure the *I*ndian nations ; and although such commission might seem out of the way of a minister of the Gospel, yet he yielded thereto on its being argued that the bringing of peace with the *I*ndians would open the way for future harvests," etc. (Penn. Arch., 1st Series, vol. III. p. 579.) Although a large price was set on the head of Post, he was fearless. "I am not afraid," he wrote, "of the *I*ndians nor the devil himself; I fear my great Creator God." (*Ibid.*, p. 542.)

However active the Germans may have been in the French and Indian War, there can be no doubt about their enthusiasm and patriotism during the Revolution. Those who have traced their history to the banks of the Rhine and the mountains of Switzerland will not be surprised at their patriotism during these trying times. A love for independence and a hatred of tyranny has ever been a distinguishing trait of Palatine and Swiss.[18] Although faithful to the English crown before the war, they had no reason to be particularly attached to it. As far back as 1748 the Swedish traveller Professor Kalm distinctly states that they had no particular feeling for England, and tells, in words that seem to be prophetic in the light of subsequent events, how one of them declared that the colonies would be in condition within thirty or fifty years to make a state for itself independent of England.[19] When

[18] " Die Freiheit ist die Luft in der Ihr geboren, das Element in dem Ihr erwachsen, der Lebensgeist der den Helvetischen Körper unterhält." (Dändliker, vol. I. p. 18.) The same "Drang nach persönlicher Unabhängigkeit" is characteristic of the Palatinate ; Riehl says that the words, " *E*ines andern Knecht soll Niemand sein, der für sich selbst kann bleiben allein," is the motto of every native in whom is Alemannic blood.

[19] Montcalm is said to have made a similar prophecy in a letter to a "cousin in France." (See Eng. Hist. Review, vol. XV. p. 128.)

the strain on the relations between the colonies and the mother country came, none were more ardent in expressing their sympathies than the Germans. On February 25, 1775, Pastor Helmuth, of the Lutheran church in Lancaster, writes that the whole land was preparing for war, nearly every man was armed, and the enthusiasm was indescribable. If one hundred men were asked for, he says, far more offered themselves and were angry if they were not taken. Even the Quakers and Mennonites took part in the exercises, and in large numbers renounced their religious principles.[20]

The importance of this testimony for our present discussion lies, of course, in the fact that Lancaster County was almost entirely inhabited by Germans. The same spirit manifested itself in Berks County, where practically the entire population was German. When news of the Tea Duty came to Reading there was great excitement, and meetings were held condemning the English. After the battle of Lexington in 1775, every township resolved to raise and drill a company.[21]

[20] A Mennonite preacher, Henry Funck, took oath to the State and did good military service ; in consequence of which he was read out of the Church. (Penn. Arch., 2d Ser., vol. III. p. 463.)

[21] Montgomery says that by July, 1775, at least forty companies were ready for active warfare. In a letter from a

At the various conventions held in Philadelphia from 1775 on, a large proportion of delegates from Berks, Lancaster, York, Northampton, and other counties were Germans. We may take as a single example the convention of 1776, of which Franklin was president. Out of 96 delegates 22 were Germans; 4 of the 8 sent by Lancaster and 3 of the 8 sent by Berks were Germans. Northampton sent 6.[22]

Such was the spirit among them. With the exception of the Mennonites and Moravians, who were opposed to war on religious grounds, the patriotic feeling was practically unanimous. Even the sects rendered assistance; the Mennonites gladly furnished money and provisions, while the Moravians were of service in many ways.[23]

---

member of Congress to Gen. Lee, dated July 23, 1776, we read : "The militia of Pennsylvania seem to be actuated with a spirit more than Roman," and again, "the Spirit of liberty reigns triumphant in Pennsylvania. (Force's Amer. Arch., 5th Ser., I. p. 532.)

In Richard Penn's *E*xamination before the House of Commons, Nov. 10, 1775, he said that there were 60,000 men fit to bear arms in Pennsylvania, and that he believed all would willingly take part in the present contest. (*Ibid.*, 4th Ser., VI. p. 126.)

[22] Among them were Muhlenberg, Hillegass, Slagle, Hubley, Kuhn, Arndt, Hartzell, Levan, Hiestand, etc.

[23] The Hon. William *E*llery of Rhode *I*sland writes in his

These facts tend to show the spirit of the Germans, who were equally earnest in putting their patriotism in operation. We have seen above how companies of militia were formed at the news from Lexington. It is a significant fact that the first force to arrive at Cambridge in 1775 was a company from York County, under Lieut. Henry Miller,[24] which had marched five hundred miles to reach its destination. Colonel William Thompson's battalion of riflemen, so styled in Washington's general orders, was enlisted in the latter part of June, 1775; eight of these companies of expert riflemen were raised in Pennsylvania. Among the captains were Michael Dou-

Diary in 1777 that the Moravians, "like the Quakers, are principled against bearing arms; but are unlike them in this respect, they are not against paying such taxes as the Government may order them to pay toward carrying on the war," etc. (Penn. Mag., vol. XI. p. 318 ff.)

In a petition to Congress the Moravians themselves say: "We hold no principle anyway dangerous or inconsistent with good government. . . . We willingly help and assist to bear public burdens and never had any distress made for taxes," etc.

President Reed of Philadelphia in a letter to Zeisberger thanked him, in the name of the whole conntry, for his services among the *I*ndians, and particularly for his Christian humanity in turning back so many war parties on their way to rapine and massacre. (De Schweinitz, Life of Zeisberger, p. 481.)

[24] Judge Pennypacker, in Penn. Mag., vol. XXII.

del of York County, George Nagel of Berks, and Abraham Miller of Northampton; the companies of Captains Ross and Smith of Lancaster were also largely made up of Germans. As the editors of the Pennsylvania Archives say, " The patriotism of Pennsylvania was evinced in the haste with which the companies of Colonel Thompson's battalion were filled to overflowing, and the promptitude with which they took up their march for Boston." [25]

All three companies of Baron von Ottendorf's corps were raised in Pennsylvania; of the German Regiment formed in 1776—which took part in Sullivan's campaign against the Indians— five companies were raised in the same State; among the captains were George and Bernard Hubley [26] of Lancaster. In all other regiments enlisted in Lancaster, Berks, York, and other counties the Germans formed a good proportion.

[25] These companies attracted much attention in the country through which they passed. Thacher in his "Military Journal of the Revolution," under date of August, 1775, says: " They are remarkably stout and hardy men ; many of them exceeding six feet in height. They are dressed in white frocks or rifle-shirts and round hats. These men are remarkable for the accuracy of their aim ; striking a mark with great certainty at two hundred yards' distance." (Penn. Arch., 2d Ser., vol. x. p. 5.)

[26] Author of one of the earliest histories of the Revolution.

Even in the city of Philadelphia the oldest German colonists formed a company of armed veterans, whose commander was over one hundred years old.[27] Unfortunately many of the rolls of Pennsylvania in the Revolution have been lost, and it is impossible to give complete statistics. We know, however, that the Quaker colony occupied a front rank in all that pertains to the war.[28] Any one who carefully goes over the extant records as recorded in the Pennsylvania Archives will convince himself that the Germans contributed their fair share of soldiers to the War of Independence.

Naturally enough we find a smaller proportion of German officers than men, especially in the higher ranks. Most of the officers from captain down in the companies formed of Germans were

[27] Graham, Hist. of the United States, vol. II. p. 531.

[28] In 1779 President Reed wrote to Washington : "We . . . hold a respectable place in the military line. We have twelve regiments equally filled with any other State and much superior to some ; we have a greater proportion raised for the war than any other . . . have been by far the greatest sufferers on the frontiers, have had more killed, more country desolated," etc. (Penn. Arch., 1st Ser., vol. VII. p. 378.) Alexander Graydon (Memoirs of a Life Chiefly Passed in Pennsylvania, p. 128) says : "Against the expected hostilities Pennsylvania had made immense exertions. . . . Had all the other provinces done as much in proportion to their ability, and the men been enlisted for the war, we might have avoided the hairbreadth escapes which ensued."

of course of the same nationality, many of them
rising afterwards in the ranks.[29]   This is true, for
instance, of the four Hiester brothers, their cousin
Major-General Joseph Hiester, Colonels Lutz,
Kichlein, Hubley, Spyker, Nagle, Eckert, Glo-
ninger, Antes, Weitzel, Zantzinger, and many
others.   The most distinguished of all, and
the only two great generals furnished by
the Germans, were Gen. Nicholas Herkimer[30]
and Gen. Peter Muhlenberg, the friend of Washington.   At the outbreak of the war the latter
was pastor of the German church at Blue Ridge,
Va., and the story is well known how one Sunday he preached on the wrongs of the colonies,
then putting off his gown, showing his uniform
beneath, ordered the drums beat at the church
door for recruits.[31]

[29] According to the Proceedings of the Penn. Ger. Soc., vol.
v. p. 18, in Northampton County 26 captains and 26 lieuten-
ants were German ; out of 2357 volunteers 2000 were Germans.

[30] The hero of Oriskany was a descendant of the New York
Palatines, a number of whom went to Tulpehocken, Berks
County, in 1723.   Of course no mention is made here of De
Kalb and Steuben, who do not come under the rubric of Penn-
sylvania Germans.

[31] This story has been rendered into verse by Thomas Buch-
anan Read :

> " Then from his patriot tongue of flame
> The startling words of freedom came," etc.

Not only in actual fighting did the Germans help the cause, but likewise in furnishing the necessary material of war, provisions, horses, wagons, etc. Lancaster, Berks, and other counties were at that time the most prosperous agricultural districts in the country. Travellers who passed through them all speak of the comfortable houses, the stately barns, and the rich fields of grain. It would be difficult to conceive what the starving army of Washington would have done had it not been for these flourishing farms. It was especially here that the non-combatant Mennonites proved their loyalty; they never denied requests for provisions. It is interesting to note how uniformly the committees appointed by Congress to look after these things were composed largely of Germans. Lancaster County seems to have done the most in this respect, then York, Berks, Northampton, and finally the English counties of Chester and Bucks.[32] We find

---

[32] We give one extract out of many which could be given from the Penn. Archives. In the call for troops on August 1, 1780, York furnished 500, Lancaster 1200, Berks 600, Northampton 500, Chester 800, Bucks 500, Philadelphia County 200, and City 300 ; of wagons Cumberland furnished 25, York 25, Lancaster 50, Berks 20, Northampton 15, Bucks 15, Philadelphia County 20, and Chester 45. (See Penn. Arch., 2d Ser., vol. III. p. 371. Cf. also Archives, 1st Ser., vol. V. pp. 301, 317, 605; vol. VI. p. 327; vol. VII. p. 567.)

ample recognition of these services in the records of the time. In Morse's American Geography published at Elizabethtown, N. J., in 1789,[33] we read: " It was from farms cultivated by these men that the American and French armies were chiefly fed with bread during the late rebellion, and it was from the produce of these farms that those millions of dollars were obtained which laid the foundation of the Bank of North America, and which fed and clothed the American army till the glorious Peace of Paris." [34]

---

[33] Quoted by Barber, History of New England, New York, New Jersey, and Pennsylvania, p. 551.

[34] Cf. also Letter of Pres. Reed to Col. Brodhead in 1779 : "The gratitude of the officers of Pennsylvania for the generous supplies afforded by the State does themselves and State great honor." (Penn. Arch., 1st Ser., vol. VII. p. 570.) One of the well-known characters of Philadelphia during the Revolution was Christopher Ludwig, Baker-General of the Continental army. At one of the provincial conventions to which he was delegate, General Mifflin proposed to open private subscriptions for the purchase of firearms. There was much opposition to this, when Ludwig thus addressed the chair : "Mr. President, I am but a poor gingerbread-baker, but you may put my name down for 200 pounds." When in 1777 he was appointed by Congress Baker-General of the army, the proposition was that he should furnish a pound of bread for a pound of flour. "No, gentlemen," he said, "I do not wish to grow rich by the war ; I have money enough. I will furnish 135 pounds of bread for every 100 pounds of flour you put into my hands." (See Penn. Mag., vol. XVI. pp. 343 ff.)

Such is a meagre outline of the part played by the Pennsylvania Germans in the Revolution. The same spirit manifests itself in all subsequent wars down to the last great rebellion. As the main discussion of this book is confined to the eighteenth century, we must content ourselves here with a few brief remarks. It is an interesting fact that just as we have already said, the first company to reach Washington at Cambridge was from York County, Pennsylvania, so, nearly one hundred years later, the first force to reach Lincoln at Washington in 1861 was a regiment composed of five companies from Reading, Allentown, Pottsville, and Lewiston,—almost entirely composed of the descendants of the German patriots of Revolutionary days.

As to the numbers engaged in the Civil War, it is not necessary here to go into details. A few facts will suffice. The population of Berks County in the sixties was about nine-tenths German; the rolls of the eight thousand soldiers furnished by this county to the Rebellion show by actual calculation about the same proportion, or, more accurately, 80 per cent of German names; this leaves out of account English names, many of which are variations of a German original. A similar computation of the rolls given in Evans' History of Lancaster County show the proportion to be somewhat less, about 60 per cent; the explanation of which, of course, lies in the fact that a larger proportion of English-speaking people inhabit that county. Although I have not extended this somewhat laborious method of ascertaining such facts to Lehigh, York, and other counties, a casual inspection of the rolls given in the various county histories leads me to believe a similar percentage would be found there.[35]

When we turn from the scenes of war and ask what have the Pennsylvania Germans done for the business, artistic, scientific, and literary development of the country, we find ourselves con-

---

[35] Following are some of the officers above the rank of captain in the Civil War who were descendants of the early German and Swiss settlers of Pennsylvania and, in a few cases, of Maryland and Virginia : Generals Beaver, Dechert, Gobin, Halderman, Hartranft, Heckman, Heintzelman, Keifer, Pennypacker, Raum, Wister, Zook, Custer, Rodenbough, Small, Sweitzer, Zeilin ; Colonels Frederick, Haupt, Levering, Shoup, Spangler, Barnitz, Runkle, Schwenk ; Majors Appel, Diller, Reinoehl, Yoder, Kress, Wilhelm, Rittenhouse ; Surgeons Egle, Kemper, Foltz, Oberly, Sternberg; Rear-Admirals Ammen, Schley ; Chaplain Ritner ; Chief Engineer Schock. For short biographies of the above see "*Officers of the Army and Navy who served in the Civil War*," ed. by Powell and Shippen.   Mention ought perhaps to be made here of Barbara Frietchie,—the heroine of Whittier's legendary poem,—who was born at Lancaster, Pa., Dec. 3, 1766, and died at Frederick, Md., Dec. 18, 1862.   For the true facts concerning her, see White's National Cyclopedia of American Biography.

fronted with a far more difficult task. In the case of politics and war we have more or less complete statistics as to the men engaged therein, and the difficulty is chiefly that of selecting such facts as will give a fair picture of the truth. In the present case we can only note the names of those who have made a national reputation in the various departments of life, leaving out of account the vast body of the middle class, which after all makes up the national life.

We have seen that the Germans were chiefly farmers, and their skill, thoroughness, and industry have made them pre-eminent in this line. Yet even in the eighteenth century there was a certain number of mechanics among them, and these carried on their trade after reaching the New World; living for the most part in the country,—for there were few towns and villages before 1750,—and carrying on farming at the same time Benjamin Rush says that the first object of the German mechanic was to become a freeholder, and that few lived in rented houses. He also says that they soon acquired the knowledge of mechanical arts which were more immediately necessary and useful to a new country.[36] This adaptability has shown itself in the

[36] Cf. also Mittelberger : ''It is a surprising fact that young people who **were** born in this land are very clever, docile, and

development of those manufactures and inventions which have made Pennsylvania so famous. One hundred and fifty years ago a glass-foundry was established by the eccentric Baron Stiegel, who also manufactured the once almost universally used ten-plate stoves;[37] the first paper-mill in the United States was built in 1690 by William Rittenhouse, a Mennonite preacher; and we already have seen how early the Germantown weavers became famous. At the present time many of the vast iron-foundries and steel plants which are found in Reading, Bethlehem, Allentown, and elsewhere have been established and are to-day owned and operated largely by men of Swiss-German descent.[38]

The Germans in the last century and up to comparatively recent times seem to have had little interest in trade;[39] yet they have given to

skilful; for many a one looks at a work of skill or art only a few times and imitates it immediately," etc.

[37] The first stoves were jamb-stoves, walled into the jamb of the kitchen fireplace, with the back projecting into the adjoining room. They bore the naïve inscription :

"Baron Stiegel ist der Mann,
Der die Ofen giessen kann."

[38] Among these "iron kings" may be mentioned H. C. Frick, Hon. John Fritz of Bethlehem, Hon. C. C. Kauffman of Lancaster Co.

[39] Proud says : "The Germans seem more adapted for agri-

the world one who is the most widely known merchant-prince in the country to-day.

In the field of learning, the Pennsylvania Germans have produced a number of men of widespread reputation, and the names of David Rittenhouse in astronomy, Joseph Leidy and Caspar Wistar in medicine, Muhlenberg in botany, Haldeman in philology and zoology, show that they have not been entirely unfruitful in the domain of scientific investigation.[40] Nor is it perhaps inappropriate to mention here the fact that the two largest telescopes in the world were given by James Lick, of a prominent family of Lebanon County, and Charles Yerkes, whose ancestors were among the first German settlers of Montgomery County.

In the fine arts we have not much to chronicle; in recent times we note a number of Pennsylvania names among well-known book-illustrators, but no one great name. So, too, in what may be called national literature,—in contradistinction to that of a purely local nature, discussed elsewhere,—in recent times the names of several

culture and the improvement of a wilderness, and the *I*rish for trade," etc. (Vol. II. p. 274.)

[40] The well-known naturalist and secretary of the Smithsonian *I*nstitution, the late Spencer F. Baird, who was born in Reading, Berks Co., was of *E*nglish, Scotch, and German descent.

place in the present discussion.[41]   In poetry, however, Bayard Taylor may be at least partly claimed, being in two lines of Pennsylvania-German blood.

[41] About the only writer who has touched the field for fiction presented by life among the Pennsylvania farmers is John Luther Long, who, in the Century Magazine for March, 1898, published a short story entitled "Ein Nix-Nutz." The young Canadian poet, Archibald Lampman, who recently died, was of Pennsylvania-German ancestry.

CHAPTER VIII.

CONCLUSION.

THE Pennsylvania Germans and their descendants have in round numbers been in America for two hundred years; they have shared in its prosperity, have borne their part in peace and war, and have contributed in no slight degree to its success. They are thoroughly American in thought, word, and deed. Most of them are completely assimilated to the Anglo-Saxon element of the American stock, and are scattered far and wide over the whole country. And yet in those communities where they are massed together they still form a more or less distinct ethnical entity,— a wedge, so to speak, thrust into the very heart of the United States, having their own language, their own peculiar religious forms,—in some cases, like the Dunkards, not to be found elsewhere in the world,—their own customs, and even their own type of figure and countenance.[1]

[1] In reading the present chapter we must bear in mind that the descendants of the early Swiss and German settlers of

Of course the German traits are not so striking to-day as they were one hundred years ago; most of the superstitions and unfortunately some of the earnest piety of our grandfathers have passed away, while in their place have come various traits of American character, some good, some bad. Yet even to-day the type is a distinct one and strikes at once every observant traveller who visits the State.

When we come to analyze the origin of these people, we find that they are composed of two great ethnical stems. As we have already seen, they came almost entirely from South Germany, especially from the Palatinate, Würtemberg, and Switzerland. The two latter countries are purely Alemannic, while the Palatinate is of Frankish basis with a more or less strong admixture of Alemannic, especially in those parts nearest the French frontiers. The Pennsylvania Germans, then, are composed of almost equal parts of both these great stems. Many of the

Pennsylvania form two distinct groups,—those who have remained on the ancestral farms, and those who have gone to the larger cities and to the States to the South and West; the two groups are probably equal in numbers. The latter group has been far more completely assimilated by their English neighbors, they have intermarried, Anglicized their names, and there are probably thousands who are unaware of their Pennsylvania-German descent.

traits given by Riehl and Dändliker,—the Frankish spirit of independence, the Schwaben-trotz of the Alemanni, the indomitable industry of both and their joy in labor, their extraordinary skill in agriculture, their frugality, honesty, and serious view of the responsibilities of life,—all these are not only cited in the works of men like Rush, Muhlenberg, and others, but are observable even to this day in the rural districts of Pennsylvania.

It is interesting to compare the character, traits, habits, customs, and ideals of the early settlers of Pennsylvania as they were in the Fatherland with those of their descendants in the years that have elapsed since their coming. Indeed in no other way can we get a true conception of the real genius of a people. No one would think of studying the character of New-Englanders without some knowledge of their Puritan ancestors as they were in England. Such a comparative study as this shows us the Pennsylvania Germans not as an isolated phenomenon in the midst of English settlements, but the bearers to the New World of another civilization, marked with their own character and customs brought from the Fatherland. We have given above some of the common traits of character; still more striking is the resemblance in customs, such as methods of farming, style of houses, love for flowers and music, affection and care for horses and cattle, religious toleration, and, perhaps more than anything else, the identity of superstitious customs and beliefs.

One trait has persisted down to the present— the strong spirit of conservatism. This has from the very beginning been blamed by their English-speaking neighbors, who a century and a half ago called them stubborn and headstrong; and even to-day the State historian is apt to call attention to the fact that the Germans are slow to move along those lines in which the Anglo-Saxon is rushing forward. This conservatism has its good and its bad sides. No doubt it would be better for some village communities to have more of the " hustle " of the West, or of the education and refinement of certain aristocratic communities of New England. On the other hand, it is certain that lack of repose is a great weakness in our national life; " Ohne Hast, ohne Rast " is an excellent motto, but Americans in general have cut the Goethean proverb into two parts, and thrown away the first. Students of ethnology like Riehl and Freytag have constantly emphasized the enormous value to a nation of a strong body of farmers.[2]

[2] Thus the former says (Bürgerliche Gesellschaft, p. 41):

It is not meant here that it is better for any particular individual to be a farmer, although it would seem that an independent life of comfort, even though one of toil, such as the Pennsylvania farmer enjoys, would be preferable to the half-slavery of shop, factory, or counting-house which, for the majority of city people, is the only prospect in life. It certainly is, however, good for a country to have a substantial, prosperous substratum of farmers, for to-day, even as yesterday and forever, the basis of national prosperity is and must remain in the tilling of the soil. I for one do not wish to see the day when the sons of the old Pennsylvania-German stock shall, like those of the Puritans of New England, be fired with ambition to migrate *en masse* to the city and to desert the homesteads of their ancestors, and especially to throw away as useless the extraordinary skill in farming which has come

"Es ruht eine unüberwindliche konservative Macht in der deutschen Nation, ein fester, trotz allem Wechsel beharrender Kern—und das sind unsere Bauern. . . . Der Bauer ist die Zukunft der deutschen Nation. Unser Volksleben erfrischt und verjüngt sich fort und fort durch die Bauern." Freytag (vol. II., 2. Abth., p. 170) says : "Auch deshalb liegt die letzte Grundlage für das Gedeihen der Völker in der einfachen Thätigkeit des Landmannes," etc.; and again: "Je reichlicher und ungehinderter neue Kraft aus den untern Schichten in die anspruchsvolleren Kreise aufsteigt, desto kräftiger und energischer wird das politische Leben des Volkes sein können."

down to them as the inheritance of thirty generations of ancestors, who have made Eastern Pennsylvania—and before that the banks of the Upper
Rhine—a veritable garden.

Not that no changes should be welcomed by
them. The farmer should share in whatever is
of service in the improvements of modern life.
Books and pictures and music and flowers char-
acterize the homes of many of our farmers to-
day; may they increase more and more! Those
who have had an opportunity of observing the
conditions of life in the rural districts for the
last twenty-five years, cannot help noticing great
changes. In some parts of Lancaster County
German is being rapidly replaced by English,
even in the home life, and in the most remote
communities. This is not so true of Lehigh,
Berks, and Northampton counties, but it seems
hardly to be doubted that the time is not far dis-
tant when the Pennsylvania-German dialect will
be a thing of the past.

Railroads, telegraphs, and trolley-cars are constantly levelling the differences between town
and country, and making the inhabitants of
Eastern Pennsylvania a more and more homo-
genous mass. A potent factor of this process is
the constant intermarrying between Germans
and their English-speaking neighbors. In no

State in the Union is there a more thorough mingling of nationalities than here. There is hardly one of the old families of Philadelphia, for instance, in which does not run English, Welsh, Scotch-Irish, Dutch, French, and German blood. This fact constantly meets the student of Pennsylvania genealogy. Away back in the eighteenth century Muhlenberg frequently speaks of the mixed marriages which he was called on to perform, and from that time down to the present the process has gone on, until to-day it is not too much to say that nearly every old family with an English or Scotch-Irish name has some strain of German blood in it, and *vice versa.*[3]

There are some who are impatient at the sug-

[3] This is true of the Morris, Shoemaker, Levering, Keen, Wistar, Keim, Ross, Evans, and many other well-known Pennsylvania families. As being of more than mere genealogical interest, a few individual examples are here given. The mother of Senator Simon Cameron was a Pfautz, his wife was a Brua; Judge Jeremiah Black, who has been called "in some respects the ablest man Pennsylvania has produced since the Revolution," was partly of German descent; we have already mentioned in other connections Spencer F. Baird, Bayard Taylor, and Archibald Lampman. The late Governor Russell of Massachusetts is said to have been a descendant of Abraham Witmer, who built in 1799 the fine old stone bridge over the Conestoga near Lancaster (see Papers of Lanc. Co. Hist. Soc., Oct. 1898). Finally, the wife of Lord Curzon, viceroy of India, belongs to the Maryland branch of Pennsylvania-German stock.

gestion that an infusion of English blood can add anything to the old-fashioned Pennsylvania-German stock; and yet, perhaps, there is no reason for this feeling. Each nation has its own characteristic features, its own strength and weakness. It seems to be universally acknowledged that the German character is marked by honesty, industry, deep religious spirit, and many other minor yet noble traits. It is this deep inwardness, as Dr. Schaff calls it, that has made the German race the founders of Protestantism, and that has produced in their midst deep thinkers and great scholars. The Anglo-Saxons have other attributes in greater measure, perhaps,—energy, individual initiative, power of self-government,—attributes which have made them the empire-builders of the world. Surely the Pennsylvania Germans should be glad to see these peculiarly English traits engrafted on their own stock; and the Anglo-Saxon American may on his side be glad to see the elements of steadiness, probity, and even conservatism mingle with the ever-increasing forward movement of American civilization. Some fifty years ago a wise German observer of American life [4] saw the advantage to be derived from this union. He says: "Could

---

[4] Francis Lieber, The Stranger in America, p. 199.

but a little of this quickness in practical percep-
tion and boldness in embarking in the most dar-
ing enterprises be engrafted on German steadiness and thoroughness, it would produce fine
fruit indeed." And we cannot close this brief
survey of an interesting subject more appro-
priately than with the words of Dr. Philip Schaff,
who, speaking of the great mission of Germans
in America, declares that they should " energet-
ically appropriate the Anglo-Saxon American
nature and its excellencies, and as far as possible
penetrate it with the wealth of their own German
temper and life."

APPENDIX.

PENNSYLVANIA-GERMAN FAMILY NAMES.

A KNOWLEDGE of family names is often of great value for the genealogist and even for the historian. This is especially true when, owing to change in environment, such names have undergone great variations of form. For this reason a brief outline of the subject is given here, so far as it concerns the group of people discussed in this book. Pennsylvania-German family names, like all other German names, may be divided into three distinct classes: first, those derived from personal names; second, those derived from occupation; and third, those derived from the place where the individual lived (including house-signs) or whence he came. In this last class may likewise be properly included nicknames, or those due to personal peculiarities, physical or mental.

The names forming the first class are by far the oldest, often running back to the early centuries of the Christian era, and in every case are of noble and dignified meaning, in which the old German love for war, belief in the northern mythology, and ideals of life, are clearly seen.[1] These personal names exist to-day in Pennsylvania, some of them but little changed; such are Albrecht=of distinguished race (P. G. Albright); Arnwald=one who rules as the eagle; Bernhard=strong as a bear; Conrad=bold in council; Dietrich=ruler of people; Eberhart=strong as a boar; Eckert=strong sword; Garman=spearman; Gebhard=generous giver (P. G. Kephart); Gerhard=strong spear; Gottschalk=servant of God; Hartman=strong man; Heidrich=of noble rank; Hildebrandt=battle-sword; Hubert=bright of intellect; Irmintraut=friend of the Walkyrie Thrudr (P. G. Ermentrout); Lühr=war-people; Reinhard=strong in counsel; Reinhold=ruler of council; Trautman=follower of the Walkyrie Thrudr.

In most cases, however, these double-stem names were shortened by dropping the second stem, whence such names as Kuhn (from Kun-

---

[1] For the meaning of German names see Heintze, Die Deutschen Familiennamen; Tobler-Meyer, Deutsche Familiennamen (Swiss); Steub, Oberdeutsche Familiennamen. In the above list of names P. G. = Pennsylvania German.

rat), Hein (from Heinrich), Ott (from Ottmann), Traut (from Trautmann), Bär, Barr (from Berhard). To these stems diminutive suffixes were added; thus from *i* we have the forms Bürki (from Burkhard), Ebi (from Ebarhard), Egli (from Agilbrecht), Hägi (from Haginbert), Lichti (from Ludger: P. G. Light), Stäheli (from Stahal), Welti (from Walther), Geissle (from Gisalhart: P. G. Yeissley); from *izo* we get Boss and Butz (from Bodomar), Dietz (from Dietrich), Fritz and Fritschi (from Friedrich: cf. Barbara Frietchie), Heintz (from Heinrich), Kuntz (from Kunrat: P. G. Koons and Kuhns), Landis, Lentz, and Lantz (from Landfrid), Lutz (from Ludwig), Seitz (from Siegfrid: P. G. Sides), Tietz (from Dietrich), Waltz (from Walther); from *iko* we get Frick (from Friedrich), Illig and the genitive Hilleges (from Hildebrand), Kündig (from Gundobert), Leidig (from Luithart); from *ilo* we get Ebli and Eberli (from Ebarhard), Bechtel (from Berchtold), Bickel (from Botger), Diehl (from Dietrich), Hirzel (from Hiruzleip: P. G. Hartzell), Hubeli (from Hugubert), Märkel and Märkli (from Markwald), Meili (from Maganhard), Nägeli (from Nagalrich), Rubli (from Hrodebert=Robert), Schnäbeli (from root Sneo= snow: P. G. Snavely); from *z* plus *l* we get Künzel (from Kunrat), Reitzel (from Ricohard = Richard), and Tietzel (from Dietrich).

From all the above forms patronymics in *mann*, *inger*, and *ler* are formed: Bausman, Beidleman, Denlinger, Dietzinger, Gehringer, Grissinger, Heintzelman, Hirtzler, Hollinger.

In addition to the purely German personal names we have also many names taken from Biblical characters and from the lives of saints: Bartel (from Bartholomaeus), Klause (Nicholas), Martin, Theiss, and Theissen (Matthias), Peters, Hensel (Johannes), Jäggi and Jäckli (Jacobus: P. G. Yeagy and Yackley), Jörg, Jörges (George: P. G. Yerrick and Yerkes), Brosius (Ambrosius), Bastian (Sebastian), Flory (Florus), Johst (Justus: P. G. Yost).

The second class of Pennsylvania-German family names are derived from the occupation of the individual; among the best known are Becker (baker), Baumgartner (orchard-grower), Brenneisen (blacksmith), Brunner (well-digger), Dreher, Trachsel, Trechsler (turner), Fischer, Gerber (tanner, currier: P. G. Garver), Glöckner (bell-ringer: P. G. Klackner), Heilman (doctor), Huber (one who owns a *hube* = small farm), Jäger (hunter), Kärcher (carter), Kohler, Koehler (coal-burner: P. G. Kaler, Cayler), Kaufman (merchant), Küfer, Küfner (cooper), Küster (sexton), Maurer (mason), Metzger (butcher), Lehmann (one under feudal tenure), Leineweber (linen-weaver), Müller, Probst (provost), Reifschneider, Riemenschneider (harness-maker), Sauter, Suter (shoemaker), Schaffner (steward), Schenck (cup-bearer), Scherer (barber), Schlegel (one who hammers), Schmidt (smith), Schneider (tailor), Schreiber (writer), Schreiner (joiner), Schütz (shooter, archer: P. G. Sheets), Schultz (mayor), Siegrist (sexton), Spengler (tin-smith), Steinmetz (stone-cutter), Tschudi (judge: Swiss), Vogt (bailiff), Wagner (wagoner), Wannemaker (basket-maker), Weber (weaver), Wirtz (landlord), Widmeyer Widmer (one who has land from church or monastery), Ziegler (brick-maker), Zimmerman (carpenter).

The first subdivision of names in the third class comprises those which denote the place where one lives or whence one comes; such are Algäuer (from the Allgau in Switzerland), Altendörfer (from village in St. Gall, Switz.), Amweg (beside the road), Amend (at end of village), Bach, Bacher, Bachman (who live near a brook), Berner (from Berne, Switz.), Basler (from Basel), Berger (lives on mountain), Beyer (a Bavarian), Biemensdörfer, Blickensdörfer (from village in Canton Zürich), Boehm (a Bohemian), Brechbühl (unploughed hill: P. G. Brightbill and

Brackbill), Breitenbach (village in Solothurn, Switz.), Brubacher (village in Zürich), Büttig-koffer (from village Büttikofen, Berne), Det-weiler (village in Canton Zürich), Diefenbach (Tiefenbach, in Canton Uri, Switz.), Diffen-dörfer (from Tiefendorf), Flückiger (village in Canton Berne), Fahrni (village in Berne), Frick (in Aargau, Switz.), Haldi, Haldeman (from Halden, common name for village in Switzer-land), Hofstetter (name of several villages in Zürich, St. Gall, and Berne), Eschelman (from Aeschi, village in Canton Berne), Imgrund (in hollow land), Imboden (in bottom-lands), Imhof (in farm-yard), Köllicker (village in Aargau), Longenecker (village in Berne), Mellinger (vil-lage in Aargau), Neuenschwander (village in Berne), Oberholtzer (several villages in Berne), Rüegsegger (Berne: P. G. Ricksecker), Schollen-berger (castle and village, Zürich), Schwab (a Swabian: P. G. Swope), Urner (from Canton Uri), Zug (Canton Zug), Zürcher (from Zürich).[2]

During the Middle Ages the houses were not numbered as now, but had signs painted on them, something after the manner of hotels at the present time. From these many names

[2] Some of these names may come from homonymous places in the Palatinate; almost all the Lancaster County family-names, however, which are derived from places, are of Swiss origin.

were derived: Bär (bear), Baum (tree), Bieber (beaver), Bischof (bishop), Engel (angel), Fasnacht (Shrove-Tuesday), Faust (fist), Fuchs (fox), Fünfrock (five-coats), Haas (hare), Hahn (rooster), Helm (helmet), Hertzog (duke: P. G. Hartsook), Holtzapfel (wild-apple), Kalb (calf: P. G. Kulp, Culp), Kaiser (emperor), König (king), Krebs (crab), Münch (monk), Oechsli (little ox: P. G. Exley), Pfaff (priest), Ritter (knight), Vogel (bird), Voegli (little bird: P. G. Feagley), Würfel (die, cube), Wolf.

Finally we have names given from personal peculiarities. Such are: Braun, Dürr (dry, thin), Fröhlich (cheerful: P. G. Frailey), Frei (free), Freytag (Friday), Gut (good), Hübschmann (handsome), Hoch (tall), Jüng (young), Kahl (bald), Klein (small), Kleindienst (small service), Krause (curly), Krumbein (crooked legs), Kurtz (short), Lang (long), Lebengut (good-liver: P. G. Livingood), Rau, Rauch (rough), Reich (rich), Roth (red), Rothrock (red-coat), Rothaermel (red-sleeve), Schwartz (black), Seltenreich (seldom rich), Weiss (white).[3]

Such were some of the names brought by the Pennsylvania Germans from the Palatinate and Switzerland to the New World. It was but nat-

---

[3] The author has written an extended treatment of this subject, which is soon to appear in the Americana Germanica.

ural that these names should undergö certain
changes in their new environments—changes
which took place from the very beginning.

An interesting illustration of the way in which
many names received an English form is seen in
the Pennsylvänia Archives, Second Series, vol.
XVII., which contains a list of the German and
Swiss settlers in Pennsylvania during the eighteenth century, the names of the vessels in which
they came, and the dates of their naturalization.
Often there are two lists given, one called the
" original list," which apparently was made by
an English-speaking person, who took down the
names as they were given to him orally, and who
spelt them phonetically.   These duplicate lists
throw a great deal of light on the pronunciation
of the names by the immigrants themselves. We
find the same person's name spelled Kuntz and
Coones, Kuhle and Keeley, Huber and Huffer,
Gaul and Kool, Vogelin and Fagley, Krautz and
Grauce, Froehlich and Frailick.   Often there are
some marvellous examples of phonetic spelling.
Thus, Albrecht Graff is written Albrake Grove,
Georg Heinrich Mertz is called Jurig Henrich
March, and Georg Born is metamorphosed into
Yerrick Burry. Thus even before the immigrant
landed the impulse toward a change of name was
given.

Sometimes the change was gradual, and we may trace many intermediate steps between the original name and its present form. Thus, for Krehbiel we have Krehbill, Grebill, Grabill, and finally Graybill. So Krumbein gives us Krumbine, Grumbein, and Grumbine, and Kuehbortz gives Kieportz and Keeports. Often members of the same family spelled their names differently. In Lancaster there once lived two brothers, one named Carpenter, the other Zimmermann, and we are told by Francis Lieber (The Stranger in America), that one family in Pennsylvania had the three forms,—Klein, Small and Little.

In some cases the changes were slight, owing to the similarity between the English and the German, as in Baker (Becker), Miller (Mueller), Brown (Braun), Weaver (Weber), Beaver (Bieber), Pepper (Pfeffer); of course Schmidt became almost at once Smith. In other cases the differences are so great that it is difficult to discover the original German form, and it is only by searching public documents and church records that the truth is found. Who, for instance, could see any connection between Seldomridge and Seltenreich, or between Rhoades and Roth? Yet nothing is surer than that in many cases these names are one and the same. It is undoubtedly true that most Pennsylvania Germans of modern

times have no conception of the changes that
have taken place. The remark of a farmer who
spelled his name Minich (with the guttural pronounced), "Oh, that Minnick is an Irishman; he
spells his name with a *k*," illustrates the ignorance of the people in regard to their own names;
for Minich and Minnick both come from the
original Muench.

In the present discussion we must bear in
mind that we are speaking of the names of those
Germans who came to America before the Revolution, and who were subject to an entirely different set of influences from the German of recent times, who changes his name consciously
and bodily into English. The names of the early
Pennsylvania Germans were changed unconsciously and according to forces with which they
had little to do. The difference between the two
is like that between the *mots savants* and the *mots
populaires* of French philology.

These German names almost all came from the
Palatinate and Switzerland. Even to-day we can
trace the Swiss origin of many, as, for instance,
Urner (from Uri), Johns (Tschantz), Neagley
(Naegeli), Bossler (Baseler). Some are of French
Huguenot origin, which by combined German
and English influence have often received a not
very elegant or euphonious form: examples are

Lemon (Le Mon), Bushong (Beauchamp), and Shunk (Jeán); the original Fierre was changed to German Faehre, and later became anglicized into Ferree.[4]

The number of different ways of spelling even the simplest names is often surprisingly large: thus, for the original Graf we find to-day Graaf, Graff, Groff, Groft, Graft, and Grove. So Baer gives us Bear, Bare, Bair. Of course the vagaries of English orthography are largely responsible for this. An interesting fact to note in this connection is the difference yet to be seen between the same names in town and country. The farmers of Pennsylvania are a conservative people, and even to-day, after nearly two hundred years of settlement in America, the people still speak their dialect. Naturally the cities were most subject to English influence, and it is there that we find the greatest changes in names. Take as an example of this the name of Kuntz (with the later forms of Kuhns and Koons) in the town and environs of Allentown. In the town proper there are recorded in the directory twenty-two Koonses,

[4] Other Huguenot names in Pennsylvania are Fortuné (Fordney), Correll, Flory, De Frehn, Farny, Ruby, Saladé, Benetum, Bevier, Bertalot, Broë (Brua), Lefevre, Levan, Erny (this name may be Swiss), Gobain, Hubert. (See Keiper, Französische Familiennamen in der Pfalz, and Geschichtsblätter des deutschen Huguenotten-Vereins.)

twelve Kuntzes, and fourteen Kuhnses; while in
the smaller villages around Allentown we find
sixty-two Kuhnses, a few Kuntzes, and no
Koonses.

There were three ways in which the change of
names took place: first, by translation; second,
by spelling German sounds according to English
methods; and third, by analogy. The former is
the most natural in cases where English equiva-
lents exist for the German; hence for Zimmermann we have Carpenter; for Steinbrenner,
Stoneburner; for Schumacher, Shoemaker; for
Seidensticker, Silkknitter; for Lebengut, Livingood; for Fuchs, Fox; for Hoch, High; and so
forth. Often only half the name is translated,
while the other half is changed phonetically, as
in Slaymaker (for Schleiermacher), Wanamaker
(for Wannemacher).

But the true field for the philologist is found
in the second class, that of English spelling of
German sounds.

The *a* in Pennsylvania German was pronounced broadly, like English *aw*, and this
sound is represented in such names as Groff and
Grove (from Graff), Swope (Schwab), Ault (Alt),
Aughey (Ache), and Rawn (Rahn). *E* was pronounced like English *a*, and this gives us the
names Staley (Stehli), Gable (Gebel), Amwake

(Amweg). *I*, pronounced *ee*, gives Reed (Rith), Sheeleigh (Schillig), also written Shelley. *U* in German has two sounds, one long and one short. The long sound is represented by *oo* in the names Hoon (Huhn), Fooks (Fuchs), Booker (Bucher), Hoover (Huber). The short sound, being unfamiliar to English ears, was lengthened, as Kootz (Kutz), Zook (Zug). Sometimes an *h* was added to indicate the lengthening of the vowel, as in Johns (Tschantz), Kuhns (Kuntz). *O* is usually retained, although sometimes spelled *oa*, as in Hoak (Hoch), Boats (Botz).

Of the diphthongs, *au* naturally is spelled *ow* or *ou*, as in Bowman (Bauman), Foust (Faust), Mowrer (Maurer).

More interesting and complicated than the above is the change in the diphthong *ei*. The regular German pronunciation of this is represented by English *i* or *y:* hence such names as Hines (Heinz), Smyser (Schmeiser), Whitesel (Weitzel), Snyder (Schneider), Tice (Theiss), Rice (Reis), Knipe (Kneipe). In the names Heilman, Weiser, and Beiler the German spelling and sound are both retained. The Pennsylvania Germans, however, pronounced *ei* as English *a*, and thus we find the names Sailor (Seiler), Graty (Kreidig), Hailman (Heilman), Espenshade (Espenscheid).

The mixed vowels were simplified, *ö* becoming *e* in Derr (Doerr), Sener (Soehner), Kelker (Koellicker), Mellick (Moehlich), *ea* in Early (Oehrle), Beam (Boehm), and *a* in Hake (Hoeck). *Ue* is long and short in German. The former givès *ee*, as in Keeney (Kuehne), Keeley (Kuchle); the latter usually gives *i*, as in Bitner (Buettner), Kindig (Kuendig), Bixler (Buechsler), Hiss (Huess), Miller (Mueller). In Sheets (Schuetz), however, short *ue* is lengthened to *ee*.

In the following names the umlaut is ignored: Stover (Stoever), Shroder (Schroeder), Shober (Schoeber).

Of course the changes undergone by consonants are not so great as in the case of vowels, yet we have some interesting phenomena. *J* is naturally changed to *y:* hence Young (Jung), Yost (Johst). *Z* becomes *s* in many names, as Curts (Kurtz), Butts (Butz). *K* and *c*, and often *g*, are interchangeable, as in Coffman (Kauffman), Cline (Kline), Capehart (Kephart = Gebhard), Grider (Kreider), Givler (Kübler). At the end of a word, *ig* usually becomes *y*, as in Leiby (Leibig), Leidy (Leidig). *T* is changed to *d* in Sides (Seitz), Road (Roth), Widmayer (Witmeyer).

H is omitted in Sener (Soehner), Cole (Kohl), Fraley (Froehlich), Leman (Lehman). *Pf* becomes simplified to f in Foutz (Pfautz), or to p in Kopp (Kopf). *B* was often pronounced by the .Pennsylvania Germans like v, and this gives rise to a large number of new names, among them being the following: Everly (Eberle), Hoover (Huber), Garver (Gerber),—also written Carver, —Whitescarver (Weissgerber), Lively (Leibly), Snavely (Schnaebele), Beaver (Bieber).

The change of *ch* into *gh* has also brought in a large number of names, as in Light (Licht), Albright (Albrecht), Hambright (Hambrecht), Slaughter (Schlachter), and the numerous class of names in baugh (bach), as Baugher (Bacher), Harbaugh (Herbach), Brightenbaugh (Breitenbach), Rodenbough (Rothenbach). *Ch* usually becomes k in the suffix *maker;* probably this is largely due to translation. Of course *sch* is simplified to *sh* or *s* in the names Slagle (Schlegel), Slatter (Schlatter), Shriner (Schreiner).

One of the most interesting of all these changes is that of *er* to *ar*, thus illustrating a phenomenon common to all languages. As the Latin *mercantem* becomes French *marchand*, as the English Derby is pronounced Darby, Clerk Clark, and so forth, so the German Gerber becomes Garver, Herbach becomes Harbaugh, Berger becomes Barger, Werfel becomes Warfel, Merkley becomes Markley, Hertzell becomes

Hartzell, and Herzog becomes Hartsook. Similar to this is the change of Spengler to Spangler.

Interesting also is the tendency to introduce an extra syllable between certain consonants, as Minich for Muench, Sherrick for Sherk, Widener for Waidner, Keneagy for Gnege, Yerrick for Jörg.

As in all language-changes, so here, analogy exerted more or less influence. When the simple spelling of foreign sounds did not produce an English-looking name, often a name which resembled the German in sound or appearance was substituted, as, for example, Rush for Roesch. This is probably the explanation of the inorganic *s* in Rhoades (for Roth), Richards (for Reichert). Probably the spelling *baugh* for *bach* may be more or less influenced by such names as Laughlin, Gough, or by American names of Dutch origin.

BIBLIOGRAPHY.[1]

THE following list contains the chief works which treat of the various topics discussed in this book. It is here given as a guide to those who wish to pursue the subject further.

GENERAL.

The Colonial Records of Pennsylvania.

Pennsylvania Archives, Phila. and Harrisburg, 1852–1900. Three Series.

The Statutes at Large of Pennsylvania, vols. 2–5. 1896–1898.

Americana Germanica. Pub. by M. D. Learned of the University of Pennsylvania.

American Historical Association, Annual Reports of. Washington, 1889–1899.

Hazard, Samuel. The Register of Pennsylvania. Phila. 1828–32.

Hallesche Nachrichten. Ed. by W. J. Mann and B. M. Schmucker. Allentown and Philadelphia, 1886, 1895.

Notes and Queries, Historical and Genealogical. Chiefly relating to interior Pennsylvania. *Ed.* by W. H. *E*gle. Harrisburg. From 1879 on.

The Pennsylvania German. *I*ssued quarterly. *Ed.* by Rev. P. C. Croll. Lebanon, Pa., 1900.

[1] This Bibliography contains only part of the sources used in the preparation of this book, sources which include not only printed material, but church and town records, traditions, and personal observation.

The Pennsylvania Magazine of History and Biography. Pub. by the Historical Society of Pennsylvania. Philadelphia. Vols. 1–22.

The Perkiomen Region, Past and Present. *E*d. by H. S. Dotterer. *I*ssued periodically. Vols. 1 and 2 have appeared. Philadelphia.

Eckhoff, A. In der neuen Heimath. 2. Ausgabe. New York, 1885.

Löher, Franz. Geschichte und Zustände der Deutschen in Amerika. 2. Ausgabe. Göttingen, 1885.

Baer, Geo. F. The Pennsylvania Germans. Myerstown, 1875.

Beidelman, William. The Story of the Pennsylvania Germans. *E*aston, 1898.

Seidensticker, *O*swald. Bilder aus der Deutsch-Pennsylvanischen Geschichte. New York, 1886.

Barber, J. W. The History and Antiquities of New England, New York, New Jersey, and Pennsylvania. 3d ed. Hartford, 1856.

Fiske, John. The Dutch and Quaker Colonies in America. Boston and New York, 1899.

Bolles, A. S. Pennsylvania, Province and State: a history from 1690 to 1790. Philadelphia and New York, 1899.

Bowen, Eli. The Pictorial Sketch-book of Pennsylvania. Philadelphia, 1852.

Burrowes, T. H. State Book of Pennsylvania. 2d ed. Philadelphia, 1847.

Egle, W. H. History of the Commonwealth of Pennsylvania. 3d ed. Philadelphia, 1883.

Fisher, S. L. The Making of Pennsylvania. Philadelphia, 1896.

—— The True William Penn. Philadelphia, 1900.

Franklin, Benjamin. An Historical Review of Pennsylvania from its *O*rigin. Philadelphia, 1812.

Gordon, T. F. The History of Pennsylvania from its Discovery by *E*uropeans to the Declaration of Independence in 1776. Philadelphia, 1829.

Histoire Naturelle et Politique de la Pensylvanie et de l'Etablissement des Quakers. Paris, 1768.

Proud, Robert. The History of Pennsylvania in North America. Philadelphia, 1797.

Sharpless, *I*saac. A Quaker *E*xperiment in Government. Philadelphia, 1898.

Egle. W. H. Pennsylvania Genealogies, chiefly Scotch-*I*rish and German. Harrisburg, 1896.

Weiser, C. Z. The Life of Conrad Weiser, the German Pioneer, Patriot, and Patron of Two Races.   2d ed. Reading, 1899.

Bean, T. W. History of Montgomery County.   Philadelphia, 1884.

Diffenderffer, F. R. The Three Earls: an Historical Sketch. New Holland, Pa., 1876.

Egle, W. H. History of the Counties of Dauphin and Lebanon. Philadelphia, 1883.

Ellis, Franklin, and *E*vans, Samuel. History of Lancaster County. Philadelphia, 1883.

Harris, Alexander. A Biographical History of Lancaster County. Lancaster, 1872.

Mombert, J. I. An Authentic History of Lancaster County. Lancaster, 1869.

Rupp, I. D. History of Lancaster County.   Lancaster, 1844.

—— History of Northampton, Lehigh, Monroe, Carbon, and Schuylkill Counties. Harrisburg, 1845.

—— History of Berks County.

Montgomery, M. L. History of Berks County.   Philadelphia, 1886.

Gibson, John. History of York County. Chicago, 1886.

Mathews, Alfred, and Hungerford, A. N. History of the Counties of Lehigh and Carbon. Philadelphia, 1884.

Walton, J. S., and Brumbaugh, M. G. Stories of Pennsylvania, or School Readings from Pennsylvania History. New York, 1897.

Scharf, J. T., and Westcott, T. History of Philadelphia. Philadelphia, 1884.

Watson, John F. Annals of Philadelphia. Philadelphia, 1830.

Bernheim, G. D. History of German Settlements in North and South Carolina. Philadelphia, 1872.

Chambers, T. F. The Early Germans of New Jersey. Dover, 1895.

Mellick, A. D. The Story of an Old Farm. Somerville, N. J., 1889.

Cobb, S. H. The Story of the Palatines : an Episode in Colonial History. New York, 1897.

Kapp, Friedrich. Geschichte der Deutschen Einwanderung in Amerika. Erster Band. Die Deutschen im Staate New York bis zum Anfang des neunzehten Jahrhunderts. Leipzig, 1868. (An abridgment of the same was published in New York, 1884.)

O'Callaghan, E. B. The Documentary History of the State of New York. Albany, 1850.

Schultz, Edward T. First Settlements of Germans in Maryland. Frederick, Md., 1896.

Strobel, P. A. The Salzburgers and their Descendants. Baltimore, 1855.

CHAPTER I.

Freytag, Gustav. Bilder aus der deutschen Vergangenheit. 5. Auflage. Leipzig, 1867.

Häusser, Ludwig. Geschichte der Rheinischen Pfalz. Heidelberg, 1856.

Heintz, P. K. Das ehemalige Fürstentum Pfalz-Zweibrücken während des dreissigjährigen Krieges. 3. Ausflage. Kaiserslautern, n.d.

Horn, W. D. von. Johannes Scherer, oder Tonsor der Wanderpfarrer in der Unterpfalz. 2. Auflage. Wiesbaden, 1869.

Illustrirte Geschichte von Würtemberg. Stuttgart, 1886.

Dändliker, Karl. Geschichte der Schweiz, in drei Bänden. Zürich, 1893–95.

Würtembergische Neujahrsblätter. Published annually. Stuttgart.

Geschichtsblätter des Deutschen Huguenotten-Vereins. Published at intervals. Magdeburg.

Robbiano, L. v. Die Rose von Heidelberg. Leipzig, 1872. (Historical novel.)

CHAPTER II.

Diffenderffer, F. R. The German *E*xodus to *E*ngland, in 1709. Lancaster, 1897. (Proceedings of Pennsylvania-German Society, vol. 7.)

Jacobs, Henry *E.* The German Emigration to America, 1709–1740. Lancaster, 1898. (Proceedings of Pennsyl-vania-German Society, vol. 8.)

Pastorius, F. D. Beschreibung von Pennsylvanien. Her-ausgegeben von Friedrich Kapp. Crefeld, 1884. (Partly translated in Old South Leaflets, No. 95.)

Penn, William. A Collection of the Works of. In two vol-umes. London, 1726.

Pennypacker, S. W. Historical and Biographical Sketches.
—— The Settlement of Germantown, Pennsylvania, and the Beginning of German *I*mmigration to North Amer-ica. Lancaster, 1899. (Proceedings of Pennsylvania-German Society, vol. 9.)

Richards, M. H. The German *E*migration from New York Province into Pennsylvania. Lancaster, 1899. (Proceedings of Pennsylvania German Society, vol 9.)

Rupp, I. D. A collection of upwards of 30,000 names of German, Swiss, Dutch, French, and other immigrants to Pennsylvania from 1727–1776. 2d ed. Philadelphia, 1880.
  (The same lists are contained in Pennsylvania Arch., 2d Series, vol. XVII.)

Sachse, J. F.　The Fatherland (1450–1700).　Philadelphia,
　1897.　(Proceedings of Pennsylvania-German Society,
　vol. 7.)
Seidensticker, Oswald.　Geschichte der Deutschen Gesell-
　schaft von Pennsylvanien, 1764–1876.　Philadelphia,
　1876.

CHAPTER IV.

Riehl, W. H.　Die Pfälzer, ein Rheinisches Volksbild.
　Stuttgart and Augsburg, 1857.
—— Land und Leute.　9. Auflage.　Stuttgart, 1894.
—— Wanderbuch als zweiter Teil zu " Land und Leute."
　3. Auflage.　Stuttgart, 1892.
—— Culturstudien aus drei Jahrhunderten.　5. Auflage.
　Stuttgart, 1896.
Meyer, E. H.　Deutsche Volkskunde.　Strassburg, 1898.
Höfler, M.　Volksmedezin und Aberglaube in Oberbayerns
　Gegenwart und Vergangenheit.　Neue Ausgabe.
　München, 1893.
Raynal, G. T.　Histoire philosophique et politique des
　Établissements et du Commerce des Européens dans les
　deux Indes.　Paris, 1778.
Journal of American Folk-lore.　Boston, 1888–1899.
Gibson, P. E.　" Pennsylvania Dutch " and Other Essays.
　2d ed.　Phila., 1874.
Rush, Benj.　An Account of the Manners of the German
　Inhabitants of Pennsylvania written in 1789.　Phila.,
　1875.
Mann, W. J.　Die gute alte Zeit in Pennsylvania.
Kalm, Peter.　Travels in North America.　London, 1812.
　(Vol. 13 of Pinkerton's Voyages and Travels).
Lettre d'un Cultivateur Américain.　Paris, 1784.
Lieber, Francis.　The Stranger in America.　Phila., 1835.
Mittelberger, Gottlieb.　Journey to Pennsylvania in the
　Year 1750, and Return to Germany in the Year 1754.
　Translated by C. T. Eben.　Phila., 1898.

La Rochefoucault-Liancourt. Voyage dans les États-Unis d'Amérique fait en 1795–1797. Paris, l'an VII.

Saxe-Weimar, Bernhard, Duke of. Travels through North America during the years 1825 and 1826. Phila., 1828.

Voyage dans la Haute Pensylvanie et dans l'État de New York (Chevalier St. Jean de Crévecœur). Paris, 1801.

Weld, I. J. Travels through the States of North America and the Provinces of Upper and Lower Canada during the years 1795–1797. London, 1800.

Croll, P. C. Ancient and Historical Landmarks in the Lebanon Valley. Phila., 1895.

CHAPTER V.

Wickersham, J. P. History of Education in Pennsylvania, Lancaster, 1886.

Smith, Wm. A Brief State of the Province of Pennsylvania (Sabin Reprints). New York, 1865.

Reichel, L. T. A History of Nazareth Hall. Phila., 1855.

Seidensticker, O. The First Century of German Printing in America, 1728–1830. Phila., 1893.

Wright, John. *Early* Bibles of America. N. Y., 1892.

Haussman, W. O. German American Hymnology, 1683–1800. (In Americana Germanica.)

Hebel, J. P. Alemannische Gedichte. Aarau, 1859.

Kobell, Franz von. Gedichte in Pfälzischer Mundart. 5. Auflage. München, 1862.

Nadler, Karl G. Fröhlich Palz, Gott erhalt's! Gedichte in Pfälzer Mundart. 2. Auflage. Kaiserslautern.

Stadler, Franz J. Die Landessprachen der Schweiz oder Schweizerische Dialektologie. Aarau, 1819.

Haldeman, S. S. Pennsylvania Dutch, a Dialect of South Germany, with an infusion of English. Phila., 1872.

Learned, M. D. The Pennsylvania-German Dialect. Part I. Baltimore, 1889.

Rauch, E. H. Pennsylvania-Dutch Hand-book. Mauch Chunk, 1879.

Fisher, H. L. 'S Alt Marik Haus Mittes in d'r Stadt. York.

—— Olden Times ; or, Pennsylvania Rural Life some fifty years ago, and other poems. York, 1888.

—— Kurzweil un' Zeitfertreib, rührende un' launige Gedichte in Pennsylvanisch-Deutscher Mundart. 2. Auflage. York, 1896.

Harbaugh, H. Harbaugh's Harfe, Gedichte in Pennsylvanisch-Deutscher Mundart. Phila., 1870.

Horne, A. R. 'Em Horn sei' Pennsylvanisch Deitsch Buch.

—— Pennsylvania-German Manual for Pronouncing, Reading, and Writing English. Kutztown. A new edition has just been published in Allentown.

Ziegler, C. C. Drauss un Deheem, Gedichte in Pennsylvänisch Deitsch. Leipzig, 1891.

Wollenweber, L. A. Gemälde aus dem Pennsylvanischen Volksleben. Phila.

CHAPTER VI.

Arnold, Gottfried. Unpartheyische Kirchen- und Ketzer-Historie. Frankfort, 1729.

Bloesch, E. Geschichte der Schweizerisch-Reformirten Kirchen. Bern, 1898–99.

Gümbel, H. Die Geschichte der Protest. Kirche der Pfalz. Kaiserslautern, 1885.

Carroll, H. K. The Religious Forces of the United States. New York, 1893.

Rupp, I. D. An Original History of the Religious Denominations at present existing in the United States. Phila., 1844.

Dubbs, J. H. Historical Manual of the German Reformed Church in the United States. Lancaster, 1885.

—— History of Reformed Church, German, in the United States. New York, 1895.

Good, J. I.   History of the Reformed Church in the United States, 1725-1792.   Reading, 1899.

Harbaugh, H.   The Life of Rev. Michael Schlatter. Phila., 1857.

—— The Fathers of the German Reformed Church in Europe and America.   6 vols.   Lancaster, 1857-72; Reading, 1881-88.   (D. Y. Heisler edited vols. 3 to 6.)

Dotterer, H. S.   Historical Notes relating to the Pennsylvania Reformed Church.   Vol. 1.   Phila., 1899.

Schaff, D. S.   The life of Philip Schaff.   New York, 1897.

Jacobs, H. E.   A History of the *E*vangelical Lutheran Church in the United States.   New York, 1897.

Documentary History of the Evangelical Ministerium of Pennsylvania and Adjacent States.   Phila., 1898.

Mann, W. J.   Life and Times of Henry Melchior Mühlenberg.   2d ed.   Phila., 1888.

Cranz, David.   The Ancient and Modern History of the Brethren . . . or Unitas Fratrum.   London, 1780.

Reichel, L. T.   The *E*arly History of the Church of the United Brethren (Unitas Fratrum), commonly called Moravians, in North America.   Nazareth, Pa., 1888.

Henry, James.   Sketches of Moravian Life and Character. Phila., 1859.

Ritter, Abr.   History of the Moravian Church in Philadelphia.   Phila., 1857.

Schweinitz, *E*dward de.   The Life of David Zeisberger. Phila., 1870.

Thompson, A. C.   Moravian Missions.   London, 1883.

Brons, A.   Ursprung, *E*ntwickelung und Schicksale der Altevangelischen Taufgesinnten oder Mennoniten.   2. Auflage.   Norden, 1891.

Egli, Emil.   Die Züricher Wiedertäufer zur Reformationszeit.   Zürich, 1878.

—— Die St. Galler Täufer.   Zürich, 1887.

Keller, Ludwig.   Die Reformation und die älteren Reformpartien.   Leipzig, 1885.

—— Ein Apostel der Wiedertäufer.   Leipzig, 1882.

Keller, Ludwig.   Geschichte der Widertäufer.   Münster, 1880.

—— Zur Geschichte der Altevangelischen Gemeinden. Berlin, 1897.

Loserth, J.   Der Communismus der Mährischen Wieder-täufer im 16. und 17. Jahrhunderte.   Wien, 1894.

—— Der Anabaptismus in Tirol.   Von seinem Anfängen bis zum Tode Jakob Huters. (1526–1536.) Wien, 1892.

—— Der Anabaptismus in Tirol vom Jahre 1536 bis zu seinem Erlöschen.   Wien, 1892.

Mannhardt, H. G. Jahrbuch der Altevangelischen Tauf-gesinnten oder Mennoniten-Gemeinden.   Danzig, 1888.

—— Festschrift zu Menno Simon's 400 jährige Geburts-tagfeier den 6. November, 1892.   Danzig, 1892.

Müller, Ernst.   Geschichte der Bernischen Täufer.   Frau-enfeld, 1895.

Nitsche, Richard.   Geschichte der Wiedertäufer in der Schweiz zur Reformationszeit.   Einsiedeln, 1885.

Staehelin, R.   Die ersten Märtyrer des Evangelischen Glaubens in der Schweiz.   Heidelberg, 1883.

Eby, B.   Kurzgefasste Kirchen-Geschichte und Glaubens-lehre der Taufgesinnten Christen.   Lancaster.

Cassel, D. K.   Geschichte der Mennoniten.   Phila., 1890.

Musser, Daniel.   The Reformed Mennonite Church. Lancaster, 1873

Ausbund, das ist: Etliche schöne christliche Lieder, etc. Germantown, 1751.

Braght, T. J. van.   Der blutige Schauplatz, oder Martyr-Spiegel der Taufgesinnten oder wahrlosen Christen, etc. Lancaster, 1814.

Philip, Dietrich. Enchiridion, oder Handbüchlein von der christlichen Lehre und Religion.   Lancaster, 1811.

Simon, Menno.   Ein Fundament und klarer Anweisung von der seligmachenden, Lehre unsers Herrn Jesu-Christi.   Lancaster, 1835.

Brumbaugh, M. G. A History of the German Baptist Brethren in Europe and America. Mt. Morris, Ill., 1899.

Mack, Alexander. A Plain View of the Rites and Ordinances of the House of God. Mt. Morris, Ill., 1888.

Chronicon Ephratense. A History of the Community of Seventh-Day Baptists at Ephrata, Lancaster Co., Pa. Translated by J. Max Hark, D.D. Lancaster, 1889.

Sachse, J. F. The German Sectarians of Pennsylvania. Philadelphia, 1899.

—— The German Pietists of Provincial Pennsylvania. Philadelphia, 1896.

Heebner, Balthasar, and Heydrick, C. Genealogical Record of the Schwenckfelders. Manayunk, 1879.

Berger, Daniel. History of the Church of the United Brethren in Christ. Dayton, O., 1897.

Wesley, John, The Works of. Vols. 3 and 4, containing his Journal. New York, 1831.

Crook, William. Ireland and the Centenary of American Methodism. London and Dublin, 1866.

Stevens, Abel. History of the Methodist Episcopal Church in the United States of America. New York, 1867.

Wakely, J. B. The Patriarch of One Hundred Years: being the Reminiscences, History, and Biography of Rev. Henry Boehm. New York, 1875.

INDEX.

WORKS ON ENGLISH HISTORY.

HENDERSON'S SIDE-LIGHTS ON ENGLISH HISTORY

Edited by ERNEST F. HENDERSON, author of "The History of Germany in the Middle Ages," etc., with 80 full-page illustrations. 300 pp. Quarto. $5.00 *net, special.*

An elaborate effort towards vitalizing the study of English history. Such topics as the personality of Queen Elizabeth; the execution of Mary Stuart; characteristic traits of Cromwell; the return of Charles II.; the Stuarts in exile; Queen Anne and the Marlboroughs, etc., are illustrated by a wealth of extracts from contemporary records, all arranged to give the effect of a continuous history. These, with the illustrations (portraits, facsimiles, caricatures, etc.), reproduced from the rarest originals, form perhaps one of the most notable bodies of illustrative material ever placed before the American student of history.

New York Tribune: "It is not unlikely that he who has dipped into this book in the early afternoon will find himself still reading when night comes . . . . a better book to put in the hands of the lover of history, whether he be a beginner or an old student, we do not know."

LEE'S SOURCE BOOK OF ENGLISH HISTORY

Edited by Dr. Guy Carleton Lee of Johns Hopkins. 600 pp. Large 12mo. $2.00, *net.*

The texts of the most important legal and constitutional documents from the earliest Saxon code to the last treaty between the British and the Boers. Besides copious illustrative material from Herodotus to date, and a working bibliography, that furnishes a clew to every important MS. and printed document upon English history. The selections are full of human interest, and equally valuable for the general reader, the student, the library, and the classroom.

GRAHAM'S ENGLISH POLITICAL PHILOSOPHY

From Hobbes to Maine. By Prof. William Graham, of Queen's College, Belfast, author of "The Creed of Science," "Socialism New and Old," etc. xxx + 415 pp. 8vo. $3.00 *net, special.*

A brilliant epitome and criticism of the chief works of the period on the subject. In this work the author endeavors first to give a compact but connected account of the political theories of the greater English political thinkers from the days of Hobbes, and secondly to distinguish what is permanently true from what is doubtful or erroneous, with the end of finally producing something like an Introduction to Political Science, resting on authority and reason combined.

Prof. John W. Burgess of Columbia: "I consider it the best work on the subject ever published in the English language. I have no doubt it will be extensively used in all the universities of this country."

HENRY HOLT & CO. 29 West 23d Street
New York

RINGWALT'S AMERICAN ORATORY

Selections, with introduction and notes, by RALPH C. RING-WALT, formerly *I*nstructor in Columbia University. 334 pp. 12mo. $1.00, *net.*

Contains Schurz's *General Amnesty*, Jeremiah S. Black's *Trial by Jury*, Phillips's *Daniel O'Connell*, Depew's *Inauguration of Washington*, Curtis's *The Leadership of Educated Men*, Henry W. Grady's *The New South*, and Beecher's *The Sepulchre in the Garden.*

F. N. Scott, *Professor in the University of Michigan:* "An extremely sensible book."

D. L. Maulsby, *Professor in Tufts College, Mass.:* "The opening essay is the best on its subject that I have seen of recent years. It shows grasp on both the early and later literature of the subject, and is thoroughly alive to modern conditions."

A. G. Newcomer, *Professor in Leland Stanford University:* "The essay on the theory of oratory is one of the most sensible and at the same time stimulating essays of the kind I have ever seen."

Ralph W. Thomas, *Professor in Colgate University:* "It is a work that the individual student should have constantly at hand."

WAGNER'S MODERN POLITICAL ORATIONS (BRITISH)

Edited by LEOPOLD WAGNER. xv + 344 pp. 12mo. $1.00, *net.*

A collection of some of the most notable examples of the political oratory of the present reign. *I*ncludes Brougham on Negro Emancipation; Fox and Cobden on the Corn Laws; Bright on the Suspension of Habeas Corpus Act; Butt and Morley on Home Rule; Gladstone on the Beaconsfield Ministry; Parnell on the Coercion Bill; and others by Beaconsfield, Russell, Randolph Churchill, Chamberlain, Macaulay, Bulwer-Lytton, Cowen, Bradlaugh, McCarthy, etc., etc.

.HENRY · HOLT & CO.   29 West 28d Street New York

VII, 1900

BARROW'S THE FORTUNE OF WAR A novel of the
last year of the American Revolution. 12mo. $1.25.

The scene is laid mainly in New York City during the British occupation, partly on one of the prison ships, and partly in the patriot camp at Morristown. The life in the headquarters of the two armies is cleverly contrasted. The story has a strong "love interest."

N. Y. Times Saturday Review: "The story is a good one, the historical data accurate, and the ways and manners of the period are cleverly presented."

The Outlook: "Miss Elizabeth Barrow has done her work, not only well, but delightfully well."

Chicago Times-Herald: "Another tale of the time of Washington, but one that is more deserving both of popular and critical appreciation than some of the much-vaunted financial successes."

Springfield Republican: "It gives a good picture of New York City as it was in the eighteenth century. . . . The story is agreeable reading."

Hartford Courant: "She has done good work in her romance; . . . it is told in a very attractive way. . . . The book is decidedly one that will entertain."

ODFREY'S THE HARP OF LIFE

Uniform with the author's "Poor Human Nature." 12mo. $1.50.

An intensely human story of an episode in the life of the first violin of an orchestra, at an *E*nglish watering-place. Miss Godfrey has again been uncommonly happy in creating a "musical atmosphere."

UCAS'S THE OPEN ROAD

A little book for wayfarers, bicycle-wise and otherwise. Compiled by E. V. LUCAS, editor of "A Book of Verses for Children." With illustrated cover-linings. Green and gold flexible covers. 12mo. $1.50.

Some 125 poems of out-door life and 25 prose passages, representing over 60 authors, including Fitzgerald, Shelley, Shakespeare, Kenneth Grahame, Stevenson, Whitman, Bliss Carman, Browning, William Watson, Alice Meynel, Keats, Wordsworth, Matthew Arnold, Tennyson, William Morris, Maurice Hewlett, *I*zaak Walton, Wm. Barnes, Herrick, Gervase Markham, Dobson, Lamb, Milton, Whittier, etc.

HENRY HOLT & CO. 29 West 28d Street
New York

CPSIA information can be obtained
at www.ICGtesting.com
Printed in the USA
BVOW06s2154040617
486033BV00008B/129/P